LANCERS FOR THE KING

A Study of the Frontier Military System of Northern New Spain,
With A Translation of the Royal Regulations of 1772.

Sidney B. Brinckerhoff

Odie B. Faulk

CARLOS III.

LANCERS for the KING

A Study of the Frontier Military System of Northern New Spain, With A Translation of the Royal Regulations of 1772.

by Sidney B. Brinckerhoff and Odie B. Faulk

FOREWORD BY KIERAN MCCARTY, O.F.M.

Arizona Historical Foundation
Phoenix   1965

Library of Congress Catalog Card Number: 65-63365

PRINTED IN ARIZONA

UNDER ATTACK   BY JACK SCHLICHTING

These Spanish presidial soldiers under Indian attack carry the arms and
equipment specified in the Royal Regulations of 1772. The leather jacket,
or *cuera*, and the leather shield were used to protect the soldiers against
Indian arrows. For offense the soldier carried a lance, a sword, two pistols,
and a carbine. This illustration of the *soldados de cuera* or leather-jacket
soldiers appeared originally on a cover of *Times Gone By*, the quarterly of
San Diego history published by the SAN DIEGO HISTORICAL SOCIETY. The
watercolor was painted by Jack Schlichting, Curator, the Serra Museum,
which is located on Presidio Hill in San Diego and often is called the birth-
place of California.

Catalonian volunteer infantry soldier of the regular Spanish army, at the Presidio of San Diego, California, 1769. Watercolor by DIANA BOVÉE in the LOS ANGELES COUNTY MUSEUM.

Soldier of the Presidio of Santa Barbara, California, about 1810. Watercolor by DIANA BOVÉE in the LOS ANGELES COUNTY MUSEUM.

DEDICATED TO
JOHN ALEXANDER CARROLL,
SEVEN YEARS A DRAGOON FOR THE CAUSE

Preface

Few areas in the United States have as interesting a history as the Southwest. The first explorers and settlers in this region were Spanish, whose story stands high in annals of courage and perserverance. In recent years much has been written about these men of Spain, most of it influenced by the pioneering efforts of Prof. Herbert Eugene Bolton of the University of California, one of America's great historians. American colonial history took on a fuller meaning through his emphasis of Spain's part in the settlement of what came to be the Southwest. However, until now no synthesis has been published of the multitude of facts about 18th century Spanish military campaigns against the Indian enemy on the northern frontier of New Spain.

The struggle to hold the northern borderland of New Spain parallels in time the colonial struggle for power and freedom on the east coast of North America which culminated in the American Revolution. While Spanish provincial soldiers may not have been as successful as the American Colonials, their story is no less dramatic. The authors of this book have attempted to focus on important points relevant to this quiet struggle in the Southwest, interpreting the problems faced by Spain in its war against the relentless Apache and Comanche enemy. The translation of an 1834 Mexican edition of the Regulations of 1772, which provided for the management and defense of the northern frontier, will help to clarify this story.

To Alfred Barnaby Thomas, author of *Teodoro de Croix and the Northern Frontier of New Spain, 1776-1783,* and Lawrence Kinnaird, author of *The Frontiers of New Spain: Nicolas de La Fora's Description, 1766-1768* the authors say, *gracias.* Without their groundwork and published studies this work would have been far more difficult. There have been other thoughtful persons to whom our gratitude is acknowledged. For his close check of the translations and his valuable suggestions, special thanks go to Prof. David M. Vigness of Texas Technological College, Lubbock, Texas. The authors likewise are deeply indebted to Dr. Arthur Woodward of Patagonia, Arizona, whose knowledge of Spanish uniforms and weapons made parts of the book possible and whose personal library provided invaluable information difficult, if not impossible, to find elsewhere. The excellent maps and special illustrations were prepared by Donald H. Bufkin of Tucson, Arizona. Special thanks are due Dr. William Wasley, Archaeologist at the State Museum, University of Arizona, Tucson, for his help in securing information about presidial architecture and construction.

For aid in securing background information and illustrations in this work, the authors are grateful to Mrs. Nova Alderson, Librarian at the Arizona Pioneers' Historical Society, Tucson; to Miss Ruth I. Mahood, Chief Curator of History at the Los Angeles County Museum; to James S. Hutchins of the Smithsonian Institution, Washington, D.C.; to James E. Serven, of Tucson, Arizona; to Charles Proctor, Museum of New Mexico, Santa Fe; to Charles DiPeso, the Amerind Foundation, Inc., Dragoon, Arizona; the Bancroft Library of the University of California; and even before all these, as well as for them, we express our thanks to the officers and staff of the Archives of the Indies for their generosity in opening that invaluable depository to American scholars.

Two modern-day "dragoons" deserve special notice: Prof. John Alexander Carroll of the University of Arizona, whose enthusiasm and support served as fuel for completion of this work; and Bert M. Fireman, Executive Vice President of the Arizona Historical Foundation, who encouraged, ably guided, and designed the publication of LANCERS FOR THE KING.

SIDNEY B. BRINCKERHOFF
ODIE B. FAULK
Tucson, Arizona

March 1965

Contents

Illustrations and Maps

Foreword

Western presses and publishing houses have run the gamut from romance to statistics on such traditional topics as the California missions, the Argonauts, the American cowboy, and ever recurring new versions of the Custer story. Yet, there is a Western hero who, in a sense, deserves to share a part in all of these epics although at the same time he is more neglected than the least of them. He is the Spanish colonial soldier in the Great West prior to the Mexican War of Independence.

He fits into any California mission story because he was garrisoned at each of twenty-one California missions. Like the Argonauts of 1849 he dreamed of mining wealth: the Cieneguilla bonanza of 1771, for example, was discovered by what primarily was a military expedition. The American cowboy, too, borrowed from his peer, the Spanish soldier, whose tradition of horsemanship dated back far before the Crusades. In the field of Indian warfare, the Spanish soldier was fighting native Americans a century before his English counterpart came to the New World, and three centuries before our Anglo-American heroes encountered their first Western Indians.

The present book, however, is not a romantic glorification of the Spanish soldier, nor shall I lead the reader into believing that it is. Rather it is a serious evaluation of the role of the Spanish soldier in one certain epoch of his long history. He was a principal participant in the extension of the Spanish empire into the lands of the American Southwest, which includes Northern Mexico.

Largely in anonymity and in numbers only a handful, the presidial soldier provided substance to what Herbert Eugene Bolton in his memorable essay, "The Mission as a Frontier Institution in the Spanish American Colonies," called *"one of the marvels in the history of the modern world . . ."* Bolton referred to Spain's quick mastery of Central America followed by ". . . rapid yet steady advance [by which she] spread her culture, her religion, her law, and her language over more than half of the two American continents . . ."

Lacking the Spanish soldier, as much as without Spanish ambition, the religious zeal of the missionaries, and significant institutions such as the mission and the presidio, this could not have been achieved. Bolton recognized as much in writing: "In the Spanish colonies the men to whom fell the task of extending and holding the frontiers were the *conquistador*, the presidial soldier, and the missionary." With brilliance and thoroughness, Professor Bolton thereupon set out to illuminate the role of the missionary, highlighting that particular role with his masterful biographical works on the remarkable Jesuit, Eusebio Francisco Kino. The epic of one romantic *conquistador*, Francisco Vásquez de Coronado, also occupied Bolton's scholarly attention, as it has numerous other authors.

Between these two magnificent examples of Spanish military leadership and Catholic religious accomplishment, the rank and file presidial soldier remained in the shadows. He was not studied as assiduously nor examined as closely as the great soldier, Coronado, and the tireless missionary - explorer - cattleman - cartographer, Father Kino.

In this book, two young authors are mindful of this important task that was recognized but not undertaken by Bolton nor by the devoted students, now his disciples, who studied reverently at his "round table." Dr. Faulk and Mr. Brinckerhoff have given us a far better look at the presidial soldier and the frontier presidio than has been possible before. They show the presidio on the Spanish Borderlands as an institution ironically anomalous to the glory of the King and Empire in New Spain.

Neglect of the Spanish soldier in writings of fact and fiction fill me personally, at one and the same time, with an articulate indignation and a quiet desperation. As a student of the Spanish mission system in the Western Hemisphere, I enjoy a daily familiarity with him and thus appreciate the intrinsic worth of the topic. As an historian, struggling to piece together the whole historical picture, I despair when I realize that the answer to many of my problems in the Spanish mission study lies in such allied studies as that of the Spanish soldier. Though certainly hinged on my own point of view, the observation, I think, is a valid one.

Why, for example, even up until the Gadsden Purchase, was the Sonora-Arizona mission system unable to reach the vicinity of present-day Phoenix, Arizona, while the New Mexico missions well over two hundred years before had reached latitudes many miles north of Phoenix? The strange, irregular pattern which the Spanish missions of western North America formed can ultimately be explained only by thorough study of the problems of Spanish soldiering. Unsolved mysteries of mission architecture, too, will find many a solution, unless I miss an educated guess, in an extensive study of the engineers and engineering involved in Spanish mining. Such mining often was conducted, as well as protected, by Spanish soldiers. Indeed, many of these miners were "lancers for the king."

In addition to the whole new body of information provided on the presidial soldier and the frontier presidio, the present study is especially valuable for the particular era under consideration and for the manner of treatment. First, it is important since this final chapter of Spanish colonial history was predominantly a military problem, especially on the northern frontier of New Spain; second, because the story is told essentially through contemporary sources. To say more would be to begin to tell the story itself, which is done most expertly in the following pages, the perusal of which I most heartily recommend to the reader.

KIERAN MCCARTY, O. F. M.
Academy of American Franciscan History
Washington, D.C.

March 1965

PART ONE

An Introduction

The Spanish era in what has come to be known as the Southwest dawned inauspiciously. In 1519 four sets of sails came over the eastern horizon —Alonso Álvarez de Piñeda was mapping the Gulf of Mexico from Florida to Yucatán at the orders of the governor of Jamaica. He made only a brief stop in the area. The few natives in Texas — Amichel, as Piñeda called it—who saw these sails could not have anticipated the long chain of events that was beginning that day. They could not have been aware that the kaleidoscope of fate had turned, and that once turned the old pattern would never be repeated. Nor nine years later could these savages have been aware of the change in their destiny, for the second appearance of Europeans in Texas was equally inauspicious.

In November of 1528, 80 survivors of the Pánfilo de Narváez expedition were thrown ashore on Galveston Island off the coast of Texas. They were more dead than alive: their bodies were exhausted, their clothing hung in tatters, and their supplies were gone. Casting themselves on the mercy of the local natives, the Karankawas, the Spaniards begged for shelter and food. Only 15 of them survived that first winter —to become slaves to the savages. After six long years of captivity, four of these survivors made their escape. Led by Álvar Núñez Cabeza de Vaca, the small party set out toward the setting sun; 18 weary months later they reached Culiacán in the northwestern part of New Spain, as Mexico then was called.

Taken to Mexico City, Cabeza de Vaca and his companions were eagerly asked had they seen any gold, any silver, any precious stones. No, Cabeza de Vaca truthfully replied, they had not, but he had heard of huge quantities of yellow metal to the north of the area he and his companions had traversed. In fact, he had heard of the fabled seven cities of gold—the Cities of Cíbola.

This response ended the quiet times for the Indians of the Southwest, years during which they had only to contend with each other and with nature. As relentlessly as night follows day, so Spaniard followed Spaniard into the area, French traders followed Spaniards, and English adventurers and American frontiersmen in turn intruded until the Indian no longer was master of his own land. True enough, this process

[1]

took three and a half centuries to be completed, but after Cabeza de Vaca and his three companions had made their long trek the old order was irrevocably altered. The day of the white man had dawned.

In 1539 Fray Marcos de Niza, guided by one of Cabeza de Vaca's quartet, made a preliminary survey of present-day Sonora and Arizona. A year later he guided a grand expedition headed by Francisco Vásquez de Coronado. But instead of fabulous wealth in Arizona and New Mexico, this expedition found only Indian pueblos. But there they heard of another fabled land, the Gran Quivíra. After wintering in upper New Mexico in 1540-1541, Coronado led his men down the Pecos River, swung northward into Texas, and reached Palo Duro Canyon near present Amarillo. There he selected a group of horsemen and pushed northward to Kansas before realizing that the Gran Quivíra, like the Seven Cities of Cíbola, was a mirage that retreated as he advanced. Somehow the gold and silver he sought were always somewhere beyond the tribe upon whom he was forcing himself at the time. In 1542 he returned to Mexico, a broken man whose golden armor was permanently tarnished.

Coronado little dreamed that during his journey to the Gran Quivíra he had come within a hundred miles of another party of Spaniards. In 1539 Hernando de Soto, another of that bold breed of conquistadors, had landed in Florida and had crossed the Southeastern United States before penetrating to the plains of Oklahoma. Returning to the Mississippi River, he contracted a fever and died, leaving command of his expedition to Luis de Moscoso de Alvarado. Moscoso thought to reach New Spain overland, but after arriving at the plains country (near present Mineral Wells, Texas) he grew discouraged and retraced his steps to the Mississippi. There his men built five crude boats, and on these they sailed down the "Father of Waters," turned westward along the gulf coast, and eventually reached Tampico.

Reports of the Coronado and DeSoto-Moscoso expeditions confirmed the fact that there were no precious minerals, no Indian tribes susceptible of exploitation, and no Mexico or Peru in the Southwest. No golden cities existed — no Cíbola, no Gran Quivíra. Therefore many years were to pass before other large-scale expeditions entered the area. The golden age of conquest and exploration had ended.

But legends die hard. There were many bold young Spaniards who believed that Coronado had not looked hard enough, that he had not searched in the right place, that wealth beyond measure lay waiting to the north. From time to time illegal expeditions, and even a few legal ones, penetrated the area, but nothing tangible resulted. Yet during the last half of the 16th century real progress was being made in New Spain. Miners and settlers gradually pushed up both coasts and through the interior, founding towns, farms, and ranches. Consolidation and slow expansion were the order of the day.

Only one exception was noted in this pattern of gradualism, and that was triggered by fear of foreign penetration. In 1578 Francis

Drake took his *Golden Hind* through the Straits of Magellan and up the west coast of South America, plundering the riches that lay in the port cities. Reaching California, which he ineffectually claimed for England, Drake turned westward and circumnavigated the globe. The Spaniards waited uneasily and in vain for Drake to return the way he had come; when he did not, they concluded that the English seadog had found the long-sought Northwest Passage, a route they were so certain existed that they had given it a name—the Straits of Anián. Spaniards had to control this passage! Therefore in 1595 a contract was awarded to Juan de Oñate, son of a silver magnate, to found settlements to the north and look for this passage. Three years later Oñate led a large party into New Mexico and established towns and farms. Then westward he went, and eastward, looking for the strait, looking for the Gran Quivíra, looking for Cíbola. Although he never found any of these goals and was removed from his governorship, Oñate left behind a permanently established province that jutted northward hundreds of miles beyond any other settled portion of New Spain.

During the first three-quarters of the 17th century, little of importance occurred in the Southwest. New Mexico grew slowly, and expeditions from it continued to make their way westward and eastward, penetrating Arizona and Texas. Then in 1680 came the Pueblo Indian revolt which almost depopulated New Mexico and forced the Spaniards to flee the wrath of aroused natives. As a result of this exodus, El Paso grew and missions were built near it for the faithful Indians who fled southward with the Spaniards. Then the reconquest began, a task that was not completed for almost two decades.

While the Spanish in New Mexico were fighting for their homes, a new threat arose to the east. Rene Robert, Sieur de la Salle, dreamed of planting a colony at the mouth of the Mississippi River to insure that all land drained by that mighty river system always would belong to France. Yet when he landed with his colonists, he found himself on the Texas coast. Despite the error, La Salle proceeded to erect Fort Saint Louis at Matagorda Bay. The Spaniards could not let such an intrusion go unchallenged. Five expeditions set out by sea from Vera Cruz, and four land expeditions entered Texas before the colony— actually only its remains—were discovered in 1689 by Alonso de León and Father Damien Massanet. Internal dissention, hostile natives, and inhospitable terrain had destroyed the French settlement for the Spaniards. To insure that the French would not return, Franciscan padres were sent to establish missions in East Texas — ill-fated missions that lasted only three short years. As no evidence of further French interest in Texas came to light, the Spaniards made no attempt to extend the East Texas mission field.

But the French had not forgotten La Salle's dream of winning the gulf coast region for France. In 1699 they established Biloxi, and in 1702 Mobile was founded. From this small beginning their settlements encroached westward until by 1713 they were at the boundary of Texas. That year from the outpost of Natchitoches, French traders set out to make contact with the Spaniards. Led by Louis Juchereau de St. Denis, a young cavalier from Canada, these traders reached San Juan Bautista, a Spanish presidio, or fort, on the Rio Grande. This event triggered a second Spanish attempt to colonize Texas. In a frenzy of fear that Texas natives would be subverted to loyalty to France, the viceroy and his council ordered East Texas colonized. Missions and presidios were to be established in the wilderness. Near the Sabine River six missions and two presidios were built in 1716, and two years later San Antonio was founded as a halfway station between the Rio Grande and the East Texas area. Shortly thereafter, La Bahía del Espíritu Santo was constructed on the coast to prevent another French landing on the Spanish coastal frontier.

While these events were transpiring in Texas, Jesuits were moving up the west coast of New Spain. Father Eusebio Francisco Kino was riding the "Rim of Christendom," planting missions and *visitas* in present-day Sonora and Arizona, laying groundwork for heroic padres who would follow in his footsteps: Juan Antonio Balthasar, Jacobo Sedelmayr, and Francisco Garcés. Arizona under the Spanish flag would never progress far beyond the mission-presidio stage, but without such men as these it would never have been settled at all during that period. Spanish civilians certainly found little to attract them there.

After this burst of activity, there followed a half century of slow expansion, consolidation, and even some contraction. In Texas and Arizona the Spaniards encountered mobile savages who did not take to the mission system which had been perfected gradually during the long advance northward from Mexico City. Lordly Comanches and fierce Apaches would not bow tamely to Spanish might, nor would they heed gentle exhortations of the padres. They had no desire to become civilized, to learn Christian doctrines, agricultural pursuits, and Spanish ways. Thus attempts to missionize these savages ended in failure, as at San Sabá where Comanches destroyed a mission built for Apaches, but never inhabited by them, and martyred the padres. Retaliatory expeditions followed such uprisings, usually with little success. Colonel Diego Ortiz Parilla mounted a large expedition in San Antonio in 1759 to punish Comanches for the raid at San Sabá, only to suffer a crushing defeat at Spanish Fort on the Red River.

In Arizona, following the Pima uprising of 1751, the presidio of Tubac was built on the Santa Cruz River, but it was a lonely outpost surrounded by hostile savages. The placement of presidios followed no master plan, nor was there an overall strategic policy for the defense of the frontier.

By 1763 the Spanish effort in the Southwest was clearly at a crossroads. That year, at the end of the Seven Years' War, Spain acquired the Louisiana Territory from France. Drastic measures were required along the northern frontier of New Spain if border provinces were to be held —if indeed Spanish officials in Mexico City and Madrid wanted them held. The province of Texas no longer was needed as a buffer against the French — the French were gone; the expensive military establishments near Louisiana could be extinguished with no loss of security from foreign intruders. Arizona, like New Mexico, was another finger jutting outward far beyond limits of settlement. No foreigners were in the area; moreover missions were having little success in the battle for souls. The Spanish treasury, overburdened by long and costly wars in Europe, would be relieved of a constant drain if such provinces were abandoned. A decision had to be reached.

The king did not act precipitously. To search for ways to economize and to seek a solution to the impasse with the barbarians along the northern frontier, the Marqués de Rubí was sent to inspect the area and make recommendations. Between 1766 and 1768 the indefatigable Rubí tramped through the region, accompanied by a trained military engineer, Nicolás de Lafora. From Sonora to Texas Rubí and Lafora studied the situation, talked with presidial commanders, merchants, civilians, and Indians, estimating the strengths and weaknesses of the missions, presidios, and civil settlements. They mapped the region, reflected on their findings, and then in 1769 presented a report in Mexico City.

True enough, the Rubí report asserted, the foreign menace was gone. But the Indian menace was greater than before. The frontier provinces should be maintained, the Marqués felt, not as a buffer against foreign encroachments, but against Indian penetrations into the interior of New Spain. A first line of defense was needed to prevent the savages from raiding farther south. Rubí proposed that existing presidios be consolidated into a cordon of defense stretching from the Gulf of California to the Gulf of Mexico. Some presidios would need to be moved, some founded, and some eliminated to achieve the consolidated defensive cordon he felt was necessary. East Texas could be abandoned, the settlers there withdrawing to San Antonio to strengthen what would become the capital city of the province. As a solution to the Indian problem, Rubí suggested an alliance *with* the Comanches *against* the Apaches; in fact, he recommended that wherever possible the Spaniards work to foment tribal warfare, but to keep all the tribes friendly to Spain! He suggested changes in the system of presidial supply. He wanted more civilians moved to the border areas. His was a comprehensive and sweeping report, one that would necessitate the expenditure of large sums but which he felt would save the frontier from depopulation.

While Rubí and Lafora were inspecting the northern provinces, another event of tremendous import occurred: in 1767 the Jesuits were ordered out of all Spanish possessions. The Jesuits had been working in the northwestern part of New Spain—present-day Sonora, Baja California, and Arizona. Coupled with reports of Russian activities in California, this withdrawal of the Jesuits made necessary a new look at Spanish policy in the region. José de Gálvez, in the capacity of visitor-general, made a tour through the area the same year that Rubí submitted his report. Gálvez, an extremely able and energetic administrator, organized and directed the colonization of Upper California, and investigated the deteriorating condition of the northern provinces. Whereas Rubí had recommended changes in the presidial system, the location of missions, and a new look at Spanish Indian policy, Gálvez recommended changes in the administrative system on the northern frontier.

At the time of the Gálvez inspection the chain of command for the Spanish empire was firmly established. The Bourbon king was a divine-right monarch, ruling much as he saw fit. What were called Spanish colonies were in fact the personal possessions of the king. These colonies, or kingdoms, were administered by viceroys, who were the alter egos of the king; in theory they performed functions in their areas that the king performed at home. However, the viceroys were not trusted fully, but were restricted by several agencies which maintained close watch on their activities and sent lengthy reports to the court. The *audiencia* was one such agency; it existed to hear complaints against the viceroys, to serve in the interim between the death of a viceroy and the arrival of his successor, to advise the viceroy on legal matters, and to act as a watchdog for the royal interest. And the royal treasurer and the archbishop kept close watch over financial and religious matters, respectively.

Gálvez in his tour of inspection saw that the Interior Provinces* were far from Mexico City, that they were not receiving the close personal attention of the viceroy, and that disaster—if not total depopulation — was imminent. What the area needed, he felt, was the close administrative attention of a field commander, one with real power, if it was to remain a settled part of the empire. He therefore recommended that military control of the frontier provinces be placed in the hands of an army brigadier whose headquarters should be on the frontier, and that this officer be given the authority to take quick action at critical moments. This commandant-general, as he would be called, would perform some of the functions of the viceroy and some of an army field commander. The viceroy quite naturally opposed changes which would divest him of part of his power, and worked against the Gálvez recommendations.

The result of the Rubí and the Gálvez reports was the issuance in 1772 of the Royal Regulations for presidios. First published in January of that year, this new plan created the Interior Provinces, consisting of Nueva Vizcaya, Sonora, Sinaloa, California, New Mexico, Coahuila, Chihuahua, Texas, Nuevo Leon, and Nuevo Santander. In charge was a commandant - inspector, not a commandant - general, functioning directly under supervision of the viceroy. The king had listened to the viceroy's protests and was willing to try less drastic changes at first. The officer selected for the post of commandant-inspector was Colonel Hugo O'Conor, an Irish mercenary long in the Spanish service and

*The capitalization will be explained in the following paragraph.

experienced on the frontier of New Spain. Manfully and energetically O'Conor worked to effect the changes ordered. East Texas was abandoned, presidios were moved, and settlements made. Alliances were sought with the Comanches, and a war of limited success was waged against the eastern Apaches. The Royal Regulations of 1772 showed that the emphasis on the northern frontier had shifted from a religious effort to a military one. As church and state were wedded under the Spanish government, the Spaniards on the frontier still came with the sword in one hand and the cross in the other, but the Royal Regulations clearly indicated that it was the sword that was in the right hand.

Yet the Interior Provinces continued to decline. By 1776 the king concluded that even more sweeping changes were necessary, so that year he established the Interior Provinces separate from the kingdom of New Spain. The area was placed under a commandant-general, who combined in his office civil, judicial, and military powers. Yet his effectiveness was limited from the first by a decision that he would be dependent upon the viceroy for supplies and troops. That proviso, coupled with wars in Europe in which Spain was engaged between 1779 and 1814, almost nullified the effectiveness of the changes that were ordered.

In the years that followed, the Interior Provinces were divided, reunited, and divided again, usually into Eastern and Western Interior Provinces. It was a hotbed of religious, civil, and commercial conflicts. The Indian problem defied lasting solution. Treaties were solemnly concluded—and solemnly broken. Officials at all levels decried the commercial stagnation of the Interior Provinces, but opposed changes which could have remedied such stagnation. In areas where ranches were numerous, the soil fertile, fish and game easily had, and wild fruits grew in profusion, the populace went hungry; where horses ran wild and belonged to any man who would catch them, soldiers and civilians were often left afoot; where danger from the Indian was so great that life was not safe, guns were allowed to rust and defenses to fall into disrepair. The area was simply too large and the problems too multitudinous; the Spanish colonial system itself was the real villain.

Yet the commandants-general worked long and hard to hold the region for Spain. As a generality they were excellent soldiers and capable administrators who achieved good results. That they succeeded at all is evidence of their ability; that they failed in part is evidence of the magnitude of the difficulties facing them. That the system erected by the Royal Regulations of 1772 reflected the best thinking of the day is evidenced by the fact that following the Independence of Mexico the northern frontier was still governed by the same regulations. Serving as the basis for defense between 1772 and 1848, the Royal Regulations thus are of tremendous significance in the history of the Southwest.

PART TWO

The Royal Regulations of 1772

in Spanish and with an English translation

On the following pages a translation into English of the Royal Regulations of 1772 appears opposite pages of the Spanish edition of the *Reglamento* as published in Mexico in 1834. The authors have endeavored to emphasize the sense and meaning of the King's instructions rather than give a literal, word-by-word translation.

The decorative border surrounding the facsimiles of pages from the *Reglamento* is typical of 18th century typography. This border is reproduced from the title page of a book of instructions for towns on the northeast frontier of New Spain, published in Nuevo Leon in 1739. An original is in the BANCROFT LIBRARY at the University of California.

[9]

REGLAMENTO

E INSTRUCCION

PARA LOS PRESIDIOS QUE SE HAN DE FORMAR

EN LA LINEA DE FRONTERA

DE LA

NUEVA ESPAÑA.

Resuelto por el Rey Nuestro Señor en cédula de 10 de Setiembre de 1772.

DE ORDEN DEL EXMO. SR. VIREY DE ESTE REINO.

MEXICO: 1834.

REIMPRESO EN LA OFICINA DE LA AGUILA, DIRIGIDA POR JOSE XIMENO,
Calle de Medinas número 6.

EL REY.

Como los presidios internos de mi reino de Nueva España se erigieron, y mantienen á tanta costa con el importante objeto de defender en aquellas fronteras las vidas y haciendas de mis vasallos, de los insultos de las naciones bárbaras, ya sea conteniéndolas y alejándolas con el escarmiento, ó ya consiguiendo por este medio y el del buen trato con los prisioneros ó rendidos, reducirlos á sociedad, y atraerlos al conocimiento de la verdadera religion; y como la experiencia (mayormente en estos últimos tiempos) acredita que lejos de lograrse tan piadosos fines, crece cada dia el número y la osadia de los indios enemigos, y se multiplican los estragos de aquellas provincias: deseando atender eficaz y prontamente al remedio de tan graves daños, asi con vigorosas providencias que escarmienten, desde luego, a las naciones bárbaras que las infestan, como con reglas sólidas y combinadas, que aseguren en adelante la quietud y pacificacion que tanto importa: he resuelto se mude la actual colocacion de presidios, segun y en los parages que espresará la instruccion que va al fin de este reglamento: que se varíe el pie, paga y gobierno económico de dichos presidios, y su tropa; como tambien crear el empleo de inspector comandante de ellos, con el objeto de que dirija y combine sus expediciones y servicio, y de que mantenga y cele la uniformidad y mas puntual observancia de lo que ordeno en los títulos siguientes.

TITULO PRIMERO.

1. Para que la tropa de presidios no experimente en adelante los daños que hasta aqui, percibiendo sus sueldos en efectos regulados por excesivos precios, cuando mi real hacienda los pagaba en dinero efectivo: prohibo desde el dia 1.° del año próximo esta práctica, con espresa declaracion, de que los gobernadores y capitanes que ahora son, y en adelante fueren de los presidios internos, no han de mezclarse, en modo alguno, en la compra de la provision y avio de sus guarniciones, bajo la pena de privacion de empleo, y de quedar inhabilitados de obtener otro en mi servicio; pero sí cuidarán muy particularmente de que la calidad de estos efectos sea buena, y sus precios equitativos.

2. El cuidado de la paga de la tropa, de los acopios necesarios para subministrarles las raciones, caballos, vestuario y montura, y de los efectos que necesitaren los soldados y sus familias, correrá con inspec-

THE KING

Whereas the interior presidios of my kingdom of New Spain were erected and are maintained at great cost, with the important objective of defending the lives and estates of my vassals on that frontier from the attacks of the barbarous tribes, either containing them and keeping them at a distance by severe punishment, or by following in this matter a policy of good treatment to those taken prisoner or who surrender, settling them in villages and attracting them to a knowledge of the true religion; and whereas experience (especially in recent times) has proven that far from succeeding with these pious measures it seems that the number and the boldness of the hostile Indians increases every day, and the ravages of these provinces are multiplying; therefore, desiring to apply quickly and effectively a remedy for these grave damages by means of vigourous measures for the immediate punishment of the barbarous nations that infest the area, as well as by definite and unified regulations to insure, in the future, their tranquility and pacification, which are so important, I have resolved that the present locations of presidios be moved in the manner and to the places stated at the end of these regulations; to vary the footing, pay, and economic management of the said presidios and their troops; and also to create the office of commandant-inspector for them, with the object that he regulate and co-ordinate their expeditions and services, and maintain and watch over the uniform and most punctual observance of that which I have ordered in the following titles:

TITLE ONE.

1. In order that the troops of the presidios do not suffer in the future, as they have in the past, the injury of receiving their salaries in merchandise sold at excessive prices while my royal treasury was paying them good money: I prohibit this practice from the first day of next year with the express command that the governors and captains who now command the interior presidios, or who may command them in the future, are not to participate in any manner whatsoever in the buying of provisions and equipment for their garrisons, under the penalty of deprivation of their commissions and of being barred from obtaining another in my service; instead, they will take particular care that the quality of such merchandise be high and the prices equitable.

2. The duty of paying the troops and of procuring the goods necessary to supply the rations, horses, uniforms, and saddles, and the effects necessary for the soldiers and their families, shall be the responsibility

For the evils that had crept into the Spanish system of presidial supply, see Max L. Moorhead, "The Private Contract System of Presidio Supply in Northern New Spain," *Hispanic American Historical Review*, XLI (February, 1961) pp. 31-54.

[13]

cion del capitan, á cargo del habilitado, que ha de nombrarse entre los subalternos de la compañia, bajo las reglas que se espresarán en adelante.

3. Para facilitar de todos modos el establecimiento importante de esta nueva planta, y que los habilitados puedan desde luego hacer los acopios de víveres, efectos y caballerias necesarias al bueno y pronto avio de las compañias presidiales: mando, que la mitad de sus situados, prefinidos en este reglamento, se les satisfaga por los oficiales reales á fines de Diciembre del presente año, ó principios del inmediato; y la otra mitad en 1.º de Julio del mismo.

4. Atendiendo á beneficiar en todo lo posible la tropa de los presidios, y que no necesite enviar sus partidas á largas distancias para cobrar los situados que se les han de satisfacer cada seis meses por mitad: ordeno, que á los cuatro de la frontera de la Sonora se les pague en la caja real de aquella provincia; que los siete siguientes de la línea, desde el de Janos al de San Saba, y el de la Nueva México, con el destacamento y auxiliares de Robledo, cobren en la de la villa de Chihuahua; y que los restantes de Santa Rosa, Moncloba, San Juan Bautista, Bahía del Espíritu Santo, y San Antonio de Bejar, con su destacamento del Arroyo del Cíbolo, perciban sus contingentes en la caja real de San Luis del Potosí, sin que por la conduccion se cargue gasto alguno á mi real hacienda, ni al comun de las compañias, respecto de deberla hacer los soldados de ella con sus propias mulas, las de los oficiales, ó alquiladas de su cuenta particular.

5. Respecto de hallarse esta tropa en continua guerra, y debiendo ser de sobresaliente calidad, y confianza: es mi voluntad, que se repute como la demas veterana de mis ejércitos, y que sus oficiales, sargentos &c. alternen en todo con los de los cuerpos arreglados, y tengan la misma obcion á los ascensos, honores, grados y recompensas, y tambien á los retiros cuando por sus heridas, achaques ó abanzada edad, no puedan continuar la fatiga de este servicio.

6. Aunque por este reglamento varía esta tropa de la demas de mi ejército en su gobierno interior, prest, vestuario, armamento y montura: declaro, que en todo lo perteneciente á la subordinacion, y leyes penales, se esté á lo que previenen las Ordenanzas generales; y para su puntual observancia, y que los oficiales, sargentos, cabos y soldados no puedan alegar ignorancia, y se enteren todos en las penas en que incurren, y en las que han de imponer: mando á mi virey, que en cuaderno aparte haga imprimir los artículos de dichas ordenanzas, que tratan estos dos puntos, de que ha de tener un ejemplar cada oficial de presidio, y existir otro en él, para que semanariamente se lea á la tropa por uno de dichos oficiales, ó á su presencia.

TITULO SEGUNDO.

Pie, paga y gratificacion de las compañias de presidios.

1. Cada uno de los quince presidios que han de formar el cordon de frontera (exceptuando el de la Bahía del Espíritu Santo) consta-

[14]

of the captain, but under the charge of a paymaster who will be named by the former from among the subaltern officers of the company, in accordance with the regulations which are set forth hereafter.

3. In order to facilitate in every way the establishment of this new position, and that the paymasters from now on can undertake the procurement of provisions, equipment, and mounts necessary for the full and prompt supplying of the presidial companies, I order that half of the pay and allowances specified in these regulations be made available to them by the royal officials on the last day of December of the present year, or the first day of next year, and the other half by the first of July of next year.

4. Intending to benefit in every possible way the troops of the presidios, and in order that it not be necessary to send parties long distances to collect the pay and supplies necessary every six months for the semi-annual disbursement: I order that the four presidios on the frontier of Sonora be paid at the royal treasury of that province; that the next seven in the cordon, from Janos to San Sabá, including that of New Mexico and the detachment and auxiliaries at Robledo, collect from the royal treasury in the Villa of Chihuahua; and that the remaining ones of Santa Rosa, Monclova, San Juan Bautista, Bahía del Espíritu Santo, and San Antonio de Béjar, with its detachment at Arroyo del Cíbolo, obtain their allowances at the royal treasury at San Luis Potosí. For the transportation of these funds nothing is to be charged to the royal treasury nor to the accounts of the companies; with regard to this, it should be done by the soldiers themselves with their own mules, those of the officers, or those hired with their own funds.

The town of Los Alamos later moved to Arizpe.

5. Because these troops are in continual warfare and must be of the highest quality and caliber, it is my pleasure that they be considered among the most reliable in my armies; their officers, sergeants, etc., are to alternate in everything with the regular troops and to have equal right to promotion, honors, rank, and pay, and also to retirement pay when because of wounds, illness, or advanced age they no longer are able to continue the hardships of service.

6. Although under this regulation these troops will differ from the rest of my army in their organization, pay, dress, armament, and mounts: I declare that everything that pertains to obedience and penal laws will be the same for them as provided in the general ordinances, and that these will be observed punctually; in order that the officers, sergeants, corporals, and soldiers cannot allege ignorance of these, and in order to advise all of them of the penalties to which they are subject and which can be imposed: I command my viceroy to print in a separate book the articles of said regulations which treat on these two points, and a copy will be sent to every presidial officer, and to every presidio, in order that it may be read to the troops once a week by the said officers, or in their presence.

The position of a Spanish presidial officer or soldier in colonial society was comparitively good. Unlike the British in their treatment of colonial American troops, the Spanish government consistently rewarded the deserving soldiers in New Spain with promotion. It is also true, however, that few *creole* Spanish presidial officers ever rose higher than the position of colonel and governor of a province. [In Mexican usage a *creole* was a person of Spanish parentage born in the Americas.]

TITLE TWO.

Footing, Pay, and Gratuities of the Presidial Companies.

1. Each one of the fourteen presidios which shall form the cordon of the frontier (except that of La Bahía del Espíritu Santo) shall

rá del capitan, teniente, alferez, capellan y cuarenta y tres plazas, inclusos un sargento y dos cabos, con mas diez indios exploradores, de los cuales se eligirá uno para cabo; el de la Bahía del Espíritu Santo, por carecer de indios á propósito para el objeto, tendrá el mismo número de oficiales que los otros, y cinco plazas mas de soldado.

2. El de San Antonio de Bejar, no comprendido en la línea, constará de un capitan, que lo será el gobernador de Tejas, de dos tenientes, un alferez, un capellan, y setenta y siete plazas, inclusos dos sargentos y seis cabos.

3. El de Santa Fé en el Nuevo México tampoco incluso en la línea, constará de su capitan, que ha de ser el gobernador de aquella provincia, dos tenientes, un alferez, un capellan y setenta y seis plazas, inclusos dos sargentos, y seis cabos.

4. La compañia volante de la colonia del Nuevo Santander quedará sobre el mismo pie y goces que hoy tiene, sin otra variacion que la de mandarla como capitan de ella el gobernador de aquella provincia, con el sueldo de tres mil pesos anuales, y la de quedar el capitan que hoy tiene, en calidad de primer teniente de ella con el sueldo que gozaba.

5. El situado de todos estos presidios es como se sigue: El de cada uno de los catorce del nuevo cordon asciende á la cantidad de 18.998 pesos 6 reales, distribuidos en esta forma:

	Ps.	Rs.
Sueldo anual del capitan............................	3.000.	
Del teniente...	700.	
Del alferez..	500.	
Del capellan...	480.	
Prest del sargento...................................	350.	
De cada uno de los cabos 300........................	600.	
De cada una de las cuarenta plazas de soldado 290......	11.600.	
De cada uno de los diez indios exploradores, á razon de 3 reales diarios.................................	1 368.	6.
Por la gratificacion de 10 pesos anuales por plaza sencilla.	400.	
Total........	18.998.	6.

El situado anual del presidio de la Bahía del Espíritu Santo del mismo cordon, importa 19.130 pesos, distribuidos asi:

	Ps.	
Sueldo anual del capitan............................	3.000.	
Del teniente...	700.	
Del alferez..	500.	
Del capellan...	480.	
Prest del sargento...................................	350.	
A la vuelta..............	5.030.	

consist of a captain, lieutenant, ensign, chaplain, and forty-three soldiers, including a sergeant and two corporals, plus ten Indian scouts, from which one shall be chosen as corporal. The presidio of La Bahía del Espíritu Santo, for lack of Indians suited to this purpose, shall have the same number of officers as the other presidios, and five more troops.

2. The presidio of San Antonio de Béjar, not included in the line, will consist of a captain, who will be the governor of Texas, two lieutenants, an ensign, a chaplain, and seventy-seven soldiers, including two sergeants and six corporals.

3. The presidio of Santa Fé in New Mexico, also not included in the line, will consist of a captain, who will also be the governor of that province, two lieutenants, an ensign, a chaplain, and seventy-six soldiers, including two sergeants and six corporals.

4. The flying company of the colony of Nuevo Santander shall remain on the same footing and with the same privileges that it presently has, varying only in that I order that the governor of that province shall be its captain, with a salary of three thousand pesos annually; the present captain will remain there in the capacity of first lieutenant with the same salary he now receives.

5. The allowance for all these presidios shall be as follows: each one of the fourteen in the new cordon shall receive the sum of 18,998 pesos, 6 reales, distributed in the following manner:

	PESOS	REALES
Annual salary of the captain...................	3,000.	
To the lieutenant.............................	700.	
To the ensign................................	500.	
To the chaplain..............................	480.	
Pay of the sergeant..........................	350.	
To each one of the corporals 300 pesos	600.	
To each one of the forty private soldiers 290 pesos.	11,600.	
To each one of the ten Indian scouts, at the rate of 3 reales daily......................	1,368.	6.
For the gratuity of 10 pesos annually for each private soldier	400.	
Total......	18,998.	6.

The annual appropriation for the presidio of La Bahía del Espíritu Santo, of the same cordon, totals 19,130 pesos, distributed as follows:

Annual salary of the captain...................	3,000.	
To the lieutenant.............................	700.	
To the ensign	500.	
To the chaplain..............................	480.	
Pay of the sergeant..........................	350.	
Carried Forward ...	5,030.	

The most numerous tribe in the vicinity was the Karankawas, a barbaric nation with whom the Spanish had little success, either military or religious.

One of the largest settlements on the frontier, Santa Fé was also the farthest north. It was founded in 1609, and was the capital of New Mexico.

Now the Mexican state of Tamaulipas.

Until approximately the end of the 19th century, the Spanish peso was worth a contemporary U. S. dollar. There were eight *reales* in a peso.

De la vuelta................ 5 030.
De cada uno de los dos cabos 300..................... 600.
De cada una de las cuarenta y cinco plazas de soldado 290. 13.050.
Por la gratificacion de 10 pesos anuales por plaza sencilla. 450.

Total........ 19.130.

El situado anual del presidio de San Antonio de Bejar será de 29.580 pesos distribuidos del modo siguiente:

Sueldo anual del gobernador de la provincia de Tejas, como tal, y como capitan de esta compañia.............. 4.000.
De cada uno de los dos tenientes 700.................... 1.400.
Del alferez.. 500.
Del capellan.. 480.
De cada uno de los dos sargentos 350.................... 700.
De cada uno de los seis cabos 300...................... 1.800.
De cada uno de los sesenta y nueve soldados 290...,.... 20.010.
Por la gratificacion del fondo comun á 10 pesos anuales por plaza.. 690.

Total........ 29.580.

El situado anual del presidio de Santa Fé en el Nuevo México será de 35.680. pesos distribuidos en esta forma:

Sueldo anual del gobernador como tal, y como capitan de esta compañia.. 4.000.
De cada uno de los dos tenientes 700.................... 1.400.
Del alferez.. 500.
Del capellan.. 480.
Prest de cada uno de los dos sargentos 350............. 700.
De cada uno de los seis cabos 300...................... 1.800.
De cada uno de los sesenta y ocho soldados 290.......... 19.720.
Por la gratificacion del fondo comun á 10 pesos por plaza.. 680.
Al teniente gobernador del pueblo del Paso al año....... 1.000.
A cada uno de los treinta vecinos auxiliares que han de reforzar el destacamento de Robledo 180................. 5.400.

Total........ 35.680.

TITULO TERCERO.

Vestuario.

1. El vestuario de los soldados de presidio ha de ser uniforme en todos, y constará de una chupa corta de tripe, ó paño azul, con una

```
                      Brought Forward ...  5,030.
To each one of the two corporals 300 pesos .....    600.
To each one of the forty-five private soldiers
    290 pesos ..............................  13,050.
For the gratuity of 10 pesos annually per
    private soldier .........................    450.
                                              _____
                      Total...... 19,130.
```

The annual appropriation for the presidio of San Antonio de Béjar shall be 29,580 pesos, distributed in this way:

```
Annual salary of the governor of the province of
    Texas, in that capacity and as captain of
    this company ...........................   4,000.
To each one of the two lieutenants 700 pesos......  1,400.
To the ensign...............................    500.
To the chaplain.............................    480.
To each one of the two sergeants 350 pesos.......    700.
To each one of the six corporals 300 pesos.......  1,800.
To each one of the sixty-nine soldiers 290 pesos.. 20,010.
For the gratuity from the common fund at 10
    pesos annually per private................    690.
                                              _____
                      Total...... 29,580.
```

The annual appropriation for the presidio of Santa Fé in New Mexico shall be 35,680 pesos, distributed in this manner:

```
Annual salary of the governor, in that capacity
    and as captain of this company ............   4,000.
To each one of the two lieutenants 700 pesos....  1,400.
To the ensign...............................    500.
To the chaplain.............................    480.
Pay of each one of the two sergeants 350 pesos...    700.
To each one of the six corporals, 300 pesos......  1,800.
To each one of the sixty-eight soldiers 290 pesos.. 19,720.
For the gratuity from the common fund at
    10 pesos per private.....................    680.
To the lieutenant governor of the pueblo of
    El Paso per year.........................  1,000.
To each one of the thirty civilian auxiliaries who
    are to reinforce the detachment of Robledo
    180 pesos................................  5,400.
                                              _____
                      Total...... 35,680.
```

TITLE THREE.

Uniforms.

1. The uniform of the presidial soldiers is to be the same for all, and will consist of a short jacket of blue woolen cloth, with

[19]

pequeña vuelta y collarin encarnado, calzon de tripe azul, capa de paño del mismo color, cartuchera, cuera y bandolera de gamuza, en la forma que actualmente las usan, y en la bandolera bordado el nombre del presidio, para que se distingan unos de otros, corbatin negro, sombrero, zapatos, y botines.

2. El vestuario no se dará nunca por entero á la compañia, sino á cada soldado las prendas que necesite por disposicion del capitan, de resulta de las revistas de ropa que ha de pasar; y para que en ningun tiempo les falte, habrá en cada presidio, al cargo y cuidado del habilitado, un suficiente repuesto de todas especies, que mandará hacer, arregladas á lo que se previene en el título de vestuario.

TITULO CUARTO.

Armamento y montura.

1. Las armas del soldado de presidio han de constar de espada ancha, lanza, adarga, escopeta, y pistolas; la espada ha de ser del tamaño y hechura que usa la demas caballería de mis ejércitos; las moharras de las lanzas han de tener un pie de toesa de largo, y pulgada y media de ancho, bien reforzadas en el centro, de suerte que formen lomo, y cortantes por ambos lados, con una vírola correspondiente, para detener la demasiada introduccion, y facilitar su retroceso y repeticion de golpes. La adarga no variará de las que usan en el dia; la escopeta, igualmente que las pistolas, estarán montadas, y tendrán las llaves á la española; el cañon de la escopeta tendrá de largo tres pies de toesa, y sobre esta proporcion se arreglará la encepadura, de modo que quede el arma equilibrada cuando se apunte. Los cañones de las pistolas no excederán de diez pulgadas; el calibre de unas y otras de diez y seis adarmes; los rastrillos de las llaves serán del mejor temple, para que resistan á la violencia del sol; los ganchos de las pistolas han de ser muy seguros y reforzados.

2. Cada uno de los indios exploradores tendrá una pistola, adarga, y lanza, ademas de su arco y carcax de flechas; y entre todos treinta caballos y cinco mulas.

3. Para que al soldado no le falte nunca el completo de su armamento habrá en cada presidio otro de repuesto, y un competente número en los arsenales de México, para irlos reponiendo segun las listas que remitiese á mi virey el inspector comandante.

4. A fin de que las armas del soldado estén siempre en el buen estado que deben, y que el armamento de repuesto pueda estar cuidado y limpio, habrá en cada compañia uno de los soldados, en calidad de armero, con la obligacion de componer lo que necesiten las armas de los soldados, y atender á la conservacion del repuesto; por lo cual se le esceptuará de toda fatiga y servicio, pero no de las ocasiones de guerra en que se emplee el todo de la compañia; se le subministrarán ó abonarán los materiales, y señalará, arbitrando el virey, aquella gratificacion que juzgare suficiente para el logro de tan importante objeto; que deberá cargarse al fondo de gratificacion.

small cuffs and a red collar, breeches of blue wool, a cloth cap of the same color, a cartridge pouch, a leather jacket, and a bandoleer of antelope hide, as is presently in use (the bandoleer to be embroidered with the name of the presidio in order to distinguish one from another), a black neckerchief, hat, shoes, and leggings.

2. The uniforms will never be given wholesale to the company, but to each individual soldier as the articles are needed, this to be determined by the captain as a result of the inspections of clothing which he is to hold; in order that the soldiers may never lack anything, there will be in each presidio, in the charge and care of the paymaster, a sufficient reserve of every type of item, which he will cause to be made in conformity with the specifications in the title on uniforms.

TITLE FOUR.

Armament and Mounts.

1. The weapons of the presidial soldier shall consist of a broad sword, lance, shield, musket, and pistols; the sword must be of the same size and style as that used by other mounted men of my armies; the lance heads are to be 32.48 centimeters [13½ inches] in length and an inch and one-half in width, well reinforced in the center in such a way as to form a ridge, and with cutting edges on both sides, each with a properly placed projection to prevent too deep a penetration and to facilitate withdrawal for additional thrusts. The shield is not to vary from those presently in use; the musket, as well as the pistols, will be for horsemen, and will have Spanish-style locks; the barrel of the musket shall be 97.44 centimeters [38½ inches] in length, the stock to be made in proper proportion in order that the weapon will be properly balanced when aimed. The barrels of the pistols shall not exceed ten inches in length; the caliber of both weapons is to be sixteen gauge [.66 caliber]; the mechanisms of the locks shall be of the best temper in order to resist the heat (violencia) of the sun; and the grips of the pistols must be very solid and reinforced.

2. Each one of the Indian scouts will have a pistol, shield, and lance in addition to his bow and quiver of arrows; and for them all, a total of thirty horses and five mules.

3. In order that no soldier shall ever lack complete armament, each presidio shall have a reserve supply, and an adequate amount will be kept in the arsenals of Mexico City to replenish them, according to the list remitted to my viceroy by the commandant-inspector.

4. So that each soldier's weapons will always be in the good condition that they should and that the reserve supply of arms be cared for and kept clean, there will be one soldier in each company designated as armorer; his duties shall be to repair when necessary the arms of the soldiers, and attend the upkeep of the reserve supply. For this work he will be exempted from all fatigue duty and service, except in time of war when the entire company is engaged. To him the materials shall be supplied and credited, and he will indicate, subject to the authority of the viceroy, the amount that he judges necessary for the fulfillment of this most important duty; the costs are to be charged to the allowance.

The uniform may be seen in the second frontispiece (p. vii) and Plate Fourteen. The three-quarters length sleeveless leather jacket was called a *cuera*. Made from four to six thicknesses of hide stitched together and opening in the front or on the sides, it was designed to stop arrows and lance thrusts. The leather leggings used were known as *botas*, and were wrapped around the lower leg and tied below the knee. They are illustrated also in Plate Fourteen.

Weapons used by the *soldados de cuera* are illustrated in Plates One to Six and Nine to Eleven. The "Spanish-style lock" specified for the guns was the *miguelet* ignition system. Because it was inexpensive, durable and simple to maintain, it was ideal for frontier service.

5. Cada soldado ha de tener existentes seis caballos, un potro, y una mula, no permitiendo el capitan que se conserve ninguno que no pueda resistir la mayor fatiga.

6. Cada soldado de los existentes en la guarnicion ha de tener uno de sus caballos de dia y noche atado, mantenido con foriage, y ensillado, y de esta observancia hago especialmente responsable al capitan y demas oficiales de la compañia, por la importancia de acudir prontamente la tropa á cualquiera salida intempestiva, rebato de enemigos, ó urgente socorro.

7. La silla (á que se reduce toda la montura del soldado) ha de ser vaquera, con las cubiertas correspondientes, llamadas mochilla, coraza, armas, coginillos, y estribos de palo cerrados, quedando de consiguiente prohibido el uso de las estriveras grandes, por impropias y perjudiciales.

TITULO QUINTO.

Distribucion de caudales, y del prest del soldado.

1. Del prest del cabo y soldado se le asistirá en dinero con dos reales diarios, para que atienda á sus gastos particulares, y los de su familia; y lo restante se retendrá en el fondo, para costear la racion diaria que ha de subministrárseles en especie, segun la necesiten, y para reemplazarle los caballos que pierda, se le inutilicen ó le deseche por inservibles el inspector, y ademas las prendas de vestuario, armamento y montura.

2. Siendo conveniente que cada cabo y soldado tenga en caja un caido de cien pesos para los fines que se espresarán en adelante, se les irá reteniendo á razon de veinte ó veinte y cinco pesos anuales, á fin de que en los cuatro ó cinco primeros años se verifique la existencia de dicho fondo, haciéndoles ver, que esta providencia tiene por objeto, si falleciese, el bien de su familia; y si se retirase por anciano, imposibilitado ó cumplido, el personal suyo.

3. Verificados estos descuentos, y el de dos por ciento que ha de percibir el habilitado por los gastos, responsabilidad y cuidado de los repuestos, y ajustada la cuenta del año con intervencion y á presencia del capitan, y del interesado ó sugeto que nombre para que la examine, se abonará en dinero de contado á cada uno lo que devengue, procurando que la entrega de estos alcances se haga en un dia mismo y á presencia de todos los soldados, á fin de que noten la diferencia de lo que percibe el gobernoso, y de buena conducta, á lo poco ó nada que le queda al desperdiciado y vicioso.

4. Al indio explorador se le asistirá en dinero con un real diario, y con la racion que necesite para sí ó su familia, si la tuviese, quedando lo demas para suplirle las armas y efectos que necesiten; y en cuanto al ajuste de su cuenta y entrega de sus alcances, se estará á lo mismo que vá prevenido para los soldados.

5. El fondo de gratificacion del presidio, á razon de diez pesos por plaza sencilla, tiene por objeto acudir á los gastos generales que ocur-

5. Each soldier shall have six serviceable horses, one colt, and one mule; the captain shall not permit any animal to be kept that cannot endure the greatest hardships.

6. Each soldier on garrison duty is to keep one of his horses tethered both day and night, maintained with forage and saddled. I hold the captain and other officers of the company especially responsible for the observance of this because of the importance of the troops responding immediately to any unexpected sortie, surprise by enemies, or urgent call for help.

7. The saddle (to which all the mounts of the soldiers will be broken) is to be of *vaquero* style, with the corrseponding covers, called *mochila*, saddle pad, leather leg guards, front mounted saddle bags, and enclosed wooden stirrups; the use of large stirrups hereafter will be prohibited since these are unsuitable and dangerous.

TITLE FIVE.

Distribution of Funds and the Pay of the Soldiers.

1. Each corporal and private will be given two reales daily in cash from his pay, to be used for his personal expenses and those of his family; the rest will remain in the common fund to pay for his daily ration, which must be purchased as needed with specie, to replace the horses that are lost, that become unusable, or that are rejected by the inspector as unserviceable, and to replace articles of uniform, armament, and harness.

2. For reasons expressed below, it is desirable that each corporal and private have in trust a reserve of one hundred pesos; therefore between twenty and twenty-five pesos will be withheld annually from his salary, in order that within the first four or five years of his service this sum will be accumulated; each soldier must be made to see that this measure has as its object the welfare of his family, or his own if he retires because of old age, incapacity, or completion of his term of service.

3. These deductions will be verified as well as the two per cent which the paymaster will receive for his expenses, responsibility, and care of reserve supplies; the year's accounts will be audited under the captain's supervision and in his presence, as well as in the presence of each interested party, or some person suggested by the interested party to examine his account; then the money due each man will be given to him. If possible, the distribution of these balances will be made on the same day and in the presence of all the soldiers so that they may note the difference between the amount received by the prudent and well-behaved, and the little or nothing that remains for the squanderer and vicious.

4. One real in cash will be given daily to each Indian scout and the ration that is necessary for himself and for his family, if he has one; the remainder will be kept to supply him with the necessary arms and supplies. In the settling of his account and the paying of balances due him, these are to be handled in the same way as provided for the soldiers.

5. The common fund of the presidio, at the rate of ten pesos per private soldier, has as its object the payment of the general expenses which

The *vaquero* saddle, forerunner of the modern American western saddle, was a practical selection. The saddle of the frontier country, it was already in use by presidio soldiers, and could be produced cheaply, in quantity, by local craftsmen. See Plates Thirteen and Fourteen for details of the saddle and equipment.

The Spanish government and other European powers during the 18th century were extremely paternalistic. At the same time, the authors of the *Reglamento* were practical men and realized the average soldier tended to be irresponsible with his pay.

ran, anticipar el coste de la racion con que ha de asistirse á los in-dios prisioneros, ó á los que se presenten á tratar de treguas, &c. y anticipar la habilitacion de los reclutas, de cuyo importe se ha de ir reintegrando con los descuentos prudentes que se les vayan haciendo; y si el recluta se hallase despues poco á propósito, y hubiese de despe-dirse ó faltase antes de haber satisfecho, quedaran las caballerias y prendas que tenga para reintegro de dicho adelantamiento al fondo; y al recluta ó soldado que quisiese comprar las prendas de vestuario, no podrán cargársele por beneficio del fondo ni otro pretesto, á mas pre-cio que el de la tasacion que se hizo al recibirlas en pago; pero las caballerías y armamento se darán con la misma equidad á los reclutas que por este medio entrarán menos empeñados; y si la deuda del sol-dado muerto y despedido, no pudiese cubrirse enteramente con sus en-seres, la pérdida que resulte la sufrirá dicho fondo, cuyo caudal ha de estar existente en caja de tres llaves, y de estas una en poder de ca-da uno de los oficiales de la compañia.

6. De dicho fondo se llevará la cuenta mas exacta y justificada, á fin de que el inspector examine su bueno y legal gobierno, y dé par-te al virey anualmente de las existencias y gastos, juntamente con lo demas relativo al estado de cada presidio y compañia.

7. Todo lo demas perteneciente á cuentas, se gobernará con la in-tervencion de los oficiales de la compañia, y en cuanto sea posible, adaptando su método al que se sigue en los cuerpos arreglados del ejército.

TITULO SESTO.

Subministracion de las prendas de vestir, y otras necesarias al avio de las familias de la tropa.

1. Con anticipacion al tiempo en que se envia por los caudales á las cajas correspondientes al pago del situado de cada presidio, dará cada soldado á su capitan, ó al que en su ausencia mandará, una lis-ta firmada de las ropas ú otros efectos que necesite ó quiera para sí, su muger, hijos y demas familia, cuyo importe no exceda de lo que pueda costear su haber, cuyas listas visará el capitan, y las pasa-rá al habilitado, para que encargue la remision de su contenido, que el soldado no podrá dejar de tomar, á menos que el capitan no ha-lle que la queja del soldado si la hubiese, es justa, y que los efectos no son absolutamente de recibo; justificado lo cual, serán de cargo del habilitado, y éste podrá hacerlo á su correspondiente.

2. Ninguno de estos efectos se ha de poder cargar al soldado á mas que al coste y costas que tenga, en lo que pondrá el capitan la ma-yor vigilancia.

3. Lo mismo se practicará con los oficiales, capellan y demas in-dividuos del presidio, si dieren sus memorias; pero por ningun caso se prohibirá que acudan libremente los mercaderes que quisiesen á ven-der sus efectos, y será libre á cualquiera individuo, ó soldado del pre-sidio, comprarles lo que les acomode, y responsable el capitan y demas oficiales de cualquiera estorsion ó mal trato que se les haga.

occur; it is also to anticipate the cost of the rations of Indian prisoners, or of those that present themselves to discuss treaties, etc., and to take care of the outfitting of recruits, an expense that may be recouped by gradual and prudent discounts. If the recruit later is found to be unfit and has to be dismissed or leaves before satisfying these expenses, his animals and belongings will be retained to reimburse the common fund for the advances made; the recruit or soldier who wishes to buy the articles of clothing will not be charged more for them than the valuation placed on them when they were taken over on account, either on the pretext of benefiting the fund or for any other reason. And the mounts and armament will be issued to the recruits without obligation and with the same equity as the usual charge. If the debt of a deceased or discharged soldier is not fully covered by the sale of his possessions, the resulting loss will be borne by the said fund. The money in the common fund is to be kept in a chest with three keys, of which one is to be carried by each of the officers in the company.

6. The most exact and certified accounting of the said fund will be kept, so that the inspector may examine its good and lawful management and give to the viceroy an annual report of its resources and expenses, together with other information relative to the state of each presidio and company.

7. Everything else pertaining to accounting will be managed under the supervision of the officers of the company, everywhere possible adapting their methods to those followed in the regular corps of the army.

TITLE SIX.

Supply of Articles of Clothing and Other Necessities for the Maintenance of the Families of the Troops.

1. In advance of the time of the sending to the respective treasuries for the funds to pay the allotment for each presidio, each soldier will give to his captain, or to whomever commands in his absence, a signed list of the clothes and other effects that he needs or wants for himself, his wife, children, and the rest of his family, the total cost not to exceed the balance due him. These lists will be countersigned by the captain and passed to the paymaster, who will place the orders as requested, so that the soldier will accept the goods unless the captain finds that the complaint of the soldier, if there is one, is justified and that the goods are not in acceptable condition. If the complaint is justified, the merchandise will become the charge of the paymaster, who will make an adjustment with his supplier.

2. None of these articles will be charged to a soldier at more than their cost; this matter the captain will give his utmost attention.

3. The same procedure will be followed with respect to the officers, chaplain, and other individuals of the presidios if they turn in a requisition. But under no circumstances will merchants who so wish be prohibited from freely entering the presidios to sell their goods, and every individual and soldier in the presidios will be free to buy from such merchants whatever they desire. Any extortion or bad treatment that may occur will be the responsibility of the captain and the other officers.

TITULO SEPTIMO.

Pólvora.

1. Siendo de tanta importancia que el soldado adquiera la mayor destreza y acierto en los tiros, de que depende el éxito de las funciones y el terror de los indios bárbaros, señaio tres libras de pólvora anuales para cada plaza, que se han de distribuir en cartuchos con bala, para que á presencia del capitan, y en los dias, y con el número de tiros que señalare, y con asistencia de los oficiales y demas de la compañia que estén en la guarnicion, se ejerciten en tirar al blanco, y será de la mayor responsabilidad del capitan el que así se verifique.

2. Como el recluta necesitará en los principios mayor frecuencia para adquirir el apunte necesario, mando se abonen siempre por el primer año que sirve, tres libras mas de pólvora (con las balas correspondientes) sobre las tres que ha de quemar como los demas soldados.

3. Prohibo que al soldado se le municione para las acciones de guerra, dándole la pólvora y balas á granel, y á este efecto habrá en el repuesto un número competente de cartuchos hechos, cuyo papel se costeará del fondo de gratificacion.

4. El repuesto de pólvora existente en cada presidio ha de ser correspondiente á ocho libras por plaza arreglada; y para que esté siempre completo, la falta que resultare justificada en la cuenta particular que se ha de llevar de los consumos, aprobada por el inspector, y á su pedimento, se suplirá de la factoría ó administracion mas inmediata, sin necesitar ni pretender otro documento de resguardo.

5. El repuesto de pólvora estará al resguardo de dos llaves, de las cuales tendrá una el capitan y otra el oficial habilitado, que llevarán juntos en cuaderno separado la razon individual de las entradas y salidas, justificacion de haberse empleado en su objeto la señalada para ejercicios y en cuanto sea posible, la consumida en acciones de guerra, debiendo cada soldado responder del uso que hizo de los cartuchos que se le entregaron á su salida.

6. A los indios exploradores se les subministrarán los cartuchos que resulten de una libra de pólvora anual, para que se ejerciten en el uso de la pistola (de que están armados) á presencia de los oficiales.

TITULO OCTAVO.

Provision de empleos.

1. Siendo tan importante que la eleccion de oficiales, y especialmente de capitanes de presidios (de cuyo acierto depende en gran parte el éxito del objeto de este establecimiento), recaiga en sugetos de conocido valor, pericia militar, aptitud y honor, y muy conveniente que desde luego se separen de estos empleos aquellos actuales en quienes concurran estas circunstancias, mando á mi virey, que inmediatamente, precedidos los mas prolijos informes, verifique la separacion de estos,

TITLE SEVEN.

Gunpowder.

1. Since it is of such importance that the soldier acquire the utmost skill and accuracy in shooting on which depends the success of their functions and the intimidation of barbarous Indians, I allot three pounds of gunpowder to each soldier annually. This will be distributed in cartridges, with bullets, so that target practice can be held in the presence of the captain on the days and with the number of shots that he designates, the officers and others of the company that are available being present; it will be a major responsibility of the captain to see that this is done.

2. As recruits will need more frequent practice at first in order to acquire the necessary proficiency, I order that in addition to the three pounds of powder given to the other soldiers they be alloted three extra pounds (with the corresponding bullets) during their first year of service.

3. I forbid that soldiers be issued an excessive quantity of powder and bullets for use in the skirmishes of war; instead, there will be kept on hand for this purpose an adequate number of ready-made cartridges, the paper for which will be purchased with money from the common fund.

4. The reserve of gunpowder kept in each presidio will be at the rate of eight pounds per regular soldier; in order that this amount always be kept, shortages in the account that are justifiable, as shown in the record of consumption that must be kept, will be made up from the nearest factory or supply depot upon the approval and at the request of the inspector; no other requisition will be necessary or required.

5. The reserve gunpowder will be safeguarded under two keys, of which the captain will have one and the regular paymaster the other; they will jointly enter in a special notebook the specific reason for each addition and withdrawal, certifying the amount used for specified exercises and, when possible, the amount consumed in engagements of war; each soldier will be required to account for the use he made of the cartridges that were issued to him when he set out.

6. The Indian scouts will be supplied annually with the cartridges that can be made from one pound of powder in order that they may practice the use of their pistols (with which they will be armed) in the presence of the officers.

TITLE EIGHT.

Assignment of Duties.

1. Since the selection of officers, especially of captains of presidios (upon whose effectiveness depends in large part the attainment of the objective of these establishments), is so important, selections will be made from those of known valor, military wisdom, ability, and honor; it would be desirable, therefore, that those now in service and not possessing these attributes be separated. I order my viceroy, following a very thorough investigation, to verify immediately the discharge of these persons,

It is evident that prior to the Regulation of 1772, few of the presidial soldiers were trained to fire their weapons, nor was there powder available for practice. In the following years conditions on the frontier also made it difficult to follow out this provision of the regulation.

There was a royal monopoly on the production of paper.

Powder seems to have been in chronic short supply on the frontier. Despite the quantity specified for reserve, it is doubtful that anywhere near the required amount was available at most presidios.

y la de los que por ancianos ó achacosos, ó por la conducta irregu‑
lar con que hayan procedido en sus mandos y manejo, considere inú‑
tiles ó perjudiciales, recomendándome los que por sus méritos se ha‑
yan constituido acreedores á que les confiera otros destinos para cuyo
desempeño se necesite menos robustéz, ó retiros correspondientes. Y
asimismo le ordeno, reemplazar con la brevedad posible, todos los em‑
pleos, eligiendo entre los oficiales de mi caballeria y dragones, ó al‑
gunos de infanteria, que por la práctica que hayan adquirido en la
guerra que se ha hecho en aquellas fronteras, sean á propósito; pero
en adelante siempre que vacare alguna compañia, tenencia ó subtenen‑
cia precederá la propuesta que le ha de pasar el inspector comandan‑
te, que proveerá interinamente con goce completo del sueldo, dándo‑
me parte para su aprobacion; teniendo presente, que para la provision
de compañias se han de preferir los tenientes de cualesquiera presidios,
que por sus distinguidas funciones, capacidad y conducta acreditada se
constituyan acreedores, y consideren á propósito para este empleo.

2. Para la provision de tenientes y alféreces, propondrá el capitan
tres sugetos en quienes concurran las calidades dichas (sin excluir los
del pais que estén en actual servicio), pasando la propuesta al inspec‑
tor comandante, y éste al virey con su aprobacion ó notas, observan‑
do lo mismo con el empleo de capellan.

3. Para el reemplazo de plazas vacantes de sargentos, hará el ca‑
pitan igual propuesta entre los que se hayan distinguido mas por su
conducta y valor, cuidando cuanto sea posible de que sepan leer y es‑
cribir, y el inspector comandante aprobará el que le parezca conve‑
niente. Las plazas de cabos las nombrará por sí el capitan.

TITULO NOVENO.

Revistas mensuales.

1. El capitan pasará mensualmente revista á su compañia, y forma‑
rá un estracto con espresion de los nombres de oficiales, sargentos, ca‑
bos, soldados y capellan; á los que se hallasen presentes pondrá al mar‑
gen una *P*: á los empleados el destino; y los empleos ó plazas vacan‑
tes se indicarán con una *V*. Los reemplazos de las vacantes del mes
anterior se justificarán por nota en dicho estracto, si fuesen de empleo
de oficial, con espresion de la fecha del cúmplase de mi virey, y cer‑
tificacion, firmada de todos los oficiales, del dia en que se le dió po‑
sesion; si de capellan, sargento ó cabo, con este último documento; y
si de soldado, copiando la partida de asiento que ha de ponerse en el
libro maestro, y el papel del tiempo de diez años que ha de darse á
todos á su entrada.

2. Para justificar las salidas, mando al capitan y oficiales subalter‑
nos de cada compañia, que bajo su palabra de honor, anoten y cer‑
tifiquen en el estracto el dia en que hubiese fallecido ó verificado su
retiro. Al oficial, sargento, cabo ó soldado, para justificacion de la va‑
cante por muerte, se añada firmada por el capellan, la copia de la par‑
tida de muertos, sacada del libro que debe tener como los párrocos

and of those who are aged or ailing, or whose conduct has been unsatisfactory in command and management, or who are considered useless or harmful; he will recommend to me those who by their merit have shown themselves worthy of less arduous duties or of suitable retirement. And at the same time I order him as quickly as possible to fill all vacant posts, selecting the new appointees from among the officers of my cavalry and dragoons, or some of infantry who by experience have some knowledge of the type of warfare that is waged on that frontier. Hereafter when a vacancy occurs in some company command, lieutenancy, or sub-lieutenancy, the matter will be handled by the commandant-inspector, who will make an interim appointment at full salary and refer the matter to me for approval; in making the selection of company commanders, it will be kept in mind to give preference to the lieutenants of the several presidios if by their distinguished records, ability and creditable conduct, they have demonstrated their merit and thus are considered qualified for such posts.

2. For the appointment of lieutenants and ensigns, the captain will propose three persons in whom are found the above-mentioned qualities (without excluding those born in the country where they are serving), submitting the nominations to the commandant-inspector, who in turn will forward them to the viceroy with his endorsement and notations; the same procedure will be observed in the selection of chaplains.

3. To fill vacant billets of sergeant, the captain will make similar nominations from among those soldiers who have most distinguished themselves by their conduct and valor, taking care as far as possible to see that they are able to read and write; the commandant-inspector will approve the one he considers best qualified. Vacancies among corporals will be filled by the captain himself.

Presidio captains had most often come from the provincial army prior to 1772. Regular Spanish army officers were consistently appointed as provincial governors, but few regulars were made available by the viceroy for presidio duty. There was little change after 1772.

TITLE NINE.

Monthly Reviews.

1. The captain will hold a monthly review of his company and will make an abstract giving the names of the officers, sergeants, corporals, soldiers, and chaplain; he will put a "P" in the margin by those that are present for their position. The offices or posts that are vacant will be indicated with a "V." The vacancies that were filled during the previous month will be noted in the abstract; if of an officer with the date of the act of my viceroy and a confirmation, signed by all of the officers, of the date when he assumed his duties; if of a chaplain, sergeant, or corporal, with the latter endorsement; and if of a soldier a copy of the enlistment entry that was put in the main record book and the ten-year papers that are given to each man upon his enlistment.

2. To justify separations, I order the captain and subaltern officers of each company, under their word of honor, to note and certify on the abstract the day the person died or retired. A vacancy caused by the death of an officer, sergeant, or soldier will be confirmed under the signature of the chaplain, copied from the record book he keeps as territorial parish priests do;

territoriales; y si fuese por retiro, se esprese la fecha del despacho en los oficiales, y en los soldados constará por nota, firmada del inspector comandante, ó de alguno de sus ayudantes, pues hasta la revista de inspeccion no ha de poder licenciarse por cumplido, ni otro motivo. Si al tiempo de la revista hubiese algun soldado á quien faltare uno ó dos meses para cumplir, y le urgiese su licencia, la dará sobre la misma revista el inspector, ó el ayudante que por su comision la pase, dispensando el dicho tiempo.

3 Estos estractos quedarán en el presidio, y se sacarán dos copias con las mismas formalidades, las cuales se dirigirán al inspector mensualmente, si fuese posible, y éste con su aprobacion remitirá una á mi virey, y al fin de cada año la general, que comprenda los doce estractos, á la caja que debe satisfacer el situado, para que haga las rebajas de las plazas vacantes en los meses que las hubiese, y los abonos correspondientes á las entradas ó reemplazos; pero la gratificacion del presidio de diez pesos por plaza, no se prorateará, sino abonará siempre por completa.

4. Siendo la palabra de honor un sagrado, á que no puede faltar el oficial sin degradarse, declaro, que si contra toda esperanza se justifica la menor alteracion en la verdad de las certificaciones que acreditan las entradas y salidas de las compañias, sean los que incurrieren depuestos de sus empleos, y despedidos de mi servicio, y ademas sufran dos años de prision en el parage ó castillo que mi virey les destinase.

TITULO DECIMO.

Trato con los indios enemigos ó indiferentes.

1. Debiendo la guerra tener por objeto la paz, y siendo el de mi mayor atencion el bien y la conversion de los indios gentiles, y la tranquilidad de los paises de Frontera, el inspector comandante, y los capitanes y tropa de presidios tendrán siempre presente, que los medios mas eficaces de conseguir tan útiles y piadosos fines, son el vigor y actividad en la guerra, y la buena fé y dulzura de trato con los rendidos, dados de paz ó prisioneros. Por tanto, la primera atencion de todos ha de ser con los indios declaradamente enemigos, mantener una viva é incesante guerra, y en cuanto sea posible atacarlos en sus mismas rancherías y terrenos; pero con los prisioneros que de estos se hagan en las funciones de guerra, prohibo todo mal trato, é impongo pena de muerte al que los matase á sangre fria, y mientras no se remitan á las cercanías de México, para que mi virey los destine como convenga. Mando se les asista con la racion de víveres diaria que se dá á los indios auxiliares; y las mugeres ó párbulos que se aprehendan, serán igualmente tratados y asistidos, procurando su conversion y enseñanza.

2. Pero habiendo acreditado la esperiencia, que la suavidad y buen trato con los prisioneros particulares es tan útil, como perniciosa la contemplacion con la nacion entera, y la facilidad de conceder paces

if the vacancy is the result of the retirement of an officer, the date is to be entered in the official records; for a soldier there will be a notation by the commandant-inspector, or by one of his assistants, for until the inspection review no one can be given a certification of completion, nor any other permit. If at the time of the review there is some soldier who lacks a month or two completing his enlistment, and there is urgent need of his release, the inspector or his authorized assistant may issue it at that review, canceling the remaining time.

3. These abstracts will remain in the presidio; two copies will be made with the usual formalities, and these will be sent to the commandant-inspector monthly, if this is possible. He will remit one copy, with his endorsement, to my viceroy. At the end of each year a general report, compiled from the twelve abstracts, will be sent to the treasury from which the presidio draws its allowance in order that deductions may be made for vacancies in the months that they occurred, and corresponding allowances made for enlistments and replacements; but the presidial common fund of ten pesos per soldier shall not be prorated, but will be retained in full always.

5. Since the word of honor is sacred and no officer without disgracing himself can be false to it, I declare that if, contrary to all my hopes, the slightest deviation from the truth is discovered in the certified statements concerning enlistments and discharges in the companies, those found guilty will be dismissed from office and discharged from my service, and moreover will suffer two years in prison in the district or fortress that my viceroy designates for them.

> Few of the corrupt presidial officers were indicted or prosecuted despite the strong statement of the Regulation. For those who were tried. punishment often was light.

TITLE TEN.

Treatment of Enemy or Indifferent Indians.

1. As the object of war should be peace, and as my main goal is the welfare and conversion of the *gentile* Indians and the tranquility of the frontier area, the commandant-inspector, the captains, and the presidial troops will always keep in mind that the most effective measures for attaining these useful and pious ends are vigor and activity in war and good faith and gentle treatment of those who surrender or are taken prisoner. Therefore the first attention of all should be directed to waging active and incessant war against the Indians who are declared enemies, where possible attacking them in their own villages and lands; but with the prisoners that are taken in war, I prohibit all bad treatment and impose the penalty of death upon those who kill them in cold blood; they shall be sent to the vicinity of Mexico City where my viceroy may dispose of them as seems convenient. I order that prisoners be assisted with the same daily rations as are given Indian auxiliaries; and the women and children that are apprehended will be treated equally and assisted, in order to procure their conversion and instruction.

> The names applied by the Spaniards to the treaty Indians and the non-treaty Indians reveal their inextricable mixing of church and state. *Apaches de razon* — reasonable Apaches— were those who made treaties and kept them. *Apaches gentiles* — heathen Apaches — w e r e those who refused to enter into covenants of peace with the Spaniards, and t h u s t h o s e against w h o m a "just" war could be waged. There were far more of the latter than the former.

2. But having been shown by experience that gentleness and good treatment with individual prisoners are useful, with the entire nation they are pernicious, as is conceding peace

ó treguas, que no sean cimentadas y seguras, mayormente á los apaches, que con distintos nombres hostilizan las fronteras, demostrando el deseo de la paz, ó reduccion cuando se hallan inferiores en fuerzas, ó atemorizados por los sucesos, y abusando despues á la primera ocasion, interpretando como debilidad la clemencia con que se les ha tratado y admitido, prohibo al inspector comandante, y á los capitanes de presidios, que puedan concederles paz; y en el caso de que la pidan con seguridades ó señales que la persuadan estable ó verdadera, ó que quieran sujetarse á mi dominacion, solo se les concederá por los capitanes una tregua ó suspension de armas (dando rehenes), por los dias suficientes para tener la confirmacion del inspector comandante, y por éste no se les alargará tampoco, sino por el tiempo necesario, para con la aprobacion de mi virey, formalizar las circunstancias y condiciones, exigiendo siempre, durante las referidas treguas, la total cesacion de hostilidades; y si se pudiere, la restitucion de prisioneros, españoles ó indios amigos.

3. Siendo de suma importancia que las naciones bárbaras se aficionen y conozcan las ventajas del cange, que de suyo trae la de conservar la vida de los prisioneros de ambas partes, y muy posible que desterrada por el interés la crueldad con que tantas veces los han asesinado, vayan dispertándose en estos indios los sentimientos de humanidad: encargo muy especialmente á mi virey, al comandante inspector y á los gobernadores y capitanes de presidios, que por los medios de estipular el cange ó cambio de prisioneros, por primera condicion de las treguas ó suspension de armas que concedan, y de guardar en él la mas escrupulosa buena fé, y por todos los oportunos, procuren establecer este uso; y en el caso de lograrse, ó tener fundadas esperanzas de ello, no remitirán los indios prisioneros á México como va prevenido; pero sí los internarán lo que baste á estorbar la facilidad de la fuga que proporciona la inmediacion de los presidios: el cange deberá hacerse hombre por hombre &c. pero si no fuese dable y hubiese de darse mas número por mis tropas, será de dos ó tres indios enemigos por cada español, y de ningun modo se entenderá esto con los indios auxiliares ó exploradores, que han de cambiarse al tanto: la solemnidad de este acto se verificará á presencia de todos los oficiales que se hallen en el parage, y certificada por ellos la relacion circunstanciada, á menos que esté presente el comandante inspector, en cuyo caso bastará su relacion firmada para que conste á mi virey.

4. Si al inspector comandante pareciere conveniente dar libertad á algun prisionero, para que llegue á noticia de las naciones enemigas el buen trato que se tiene con los rendidos, al paso que ya conocen el vigor con que se les hace la guerra, podrá ejecutarlo.

5. Las presas que se hicieren sobre los enemigos, siendo de caballos, mulas, ganados, víveres ú otros efectos de los pocos que poseen, se repartirán solo entre los soldados é indios exploradores ó auxiliares que se hallaren en la accion, en premio de su fatiga; pero por ningun caso las personas con quienes debe practicarse lo prevenido arriba.

6. Con las naciones que se mantienen quietas ó neutrales, se conservará el mejor trato y correspondencia, disimulándoles algunas faltas ó

or treaties which are not certain or secure. Especially is this true with the Apaches, who under different names ravage the frontiers. When their forces are inferior or they are overwhelmed by our victories, they profess a desire for peace; afterwards, they abuse our clemency at the first opportunity, interpreting as weakness the kind treatment they were given. I prohibit the commandant-inspector and the captains of presidios from granting them peace; in case they ask for it with assurances and with indications that their request is genuine and that they will submit to my authority, the captain will concede them only a truce, or suspension of fighting (with hostages), for the number of days necessary to seek confirmation from the commandant-inspector; and he is not to extend it any longer than the time necessary for obtaining the approval of my viceroy and for formalizing the terms and conditions, demanding always during the aforesaid truce the total cessation of hostilities and, if possible, the restitution of Spanish and friendly Indian prisoners.

3. Since it is of such importance that the barbarous nations come to like and to recognize the advantages of exchanges, which in themselves preserve the lives of the prisoners on both sides, and since it is possible that self-interest will destroy the cruelty that so many times has led them to murder their captives and awaken in them sentiments of humanity, I especially charge my viceroy, the commandant-inspector, and the governors and captains of presidios to stipulate the release or exchange of prisoners as the first condition of the treaties or suspensions of fighting that they concede, and to abide by these with the most scrupulous good faith, and at every opportunity work to establish this custom. In case of success, or the well-founded hope of it, Indian prisoners will not be remitted to Mexico City, as provided above, but will be interned sufficiently far from the vicinity of the presidios as to hinder escape. The exchange will be man for man, etc., but if this is not possible and it is necessary to give more for my troops, it will be two or three Indians for each Spaniard. By no means will this extend to Indian auxiliaries or scouts, who will be exchanged at an equal ratio. The solemnity of such exchanges will be verified by the presence of all the officers that are in the vicinity and they will certify the resulting report, unless the commandant-inspector is present in which case his signature alone will suffice to my viceroy.

4. If the commandant-inspector feels it advisable to set a prisoner at liberty to spread among enemy tribes the news of our good treatment of prisoners and it happens that they know the vigor with which we make war, he is empowered to do so.

5. The spoils that are taken from enemies, whether of horses, mules, cattle, provisions, or other effects of the little that they possess, are to be divided solely between the soldiers and Indian scouts and auxiliaries that took part in the action as a reward for their struggles; but in no case is this to apply to the persons to whom the preceding instructions apply.

6. With the nations that remain quiet or neutral there will be maintained the best treatment and communication, overlooking some of their faults and

Of all Indians who plagued the Spanish frontier, the Apaches were the most difficult to subdue. After 1772 the Spaniards met with a little more success, especially against the western bands in Arizona.

This booty system undoubtedly served as an incentive to the presidio troops and may have been an inducement in recruiting soldiers.

leves excesos, y procurando inducirlos con el buen ejemplo y persuacion á que admitan misioneros, y se reduzcan á mi dominacion: si alguna vez hicieren (como suelen) robo de caballada, ú otro exceso que no conviene disimular, y requeridos no los restituyesen, se les obligará con la fuerza, haciéndoles el menos daño que sea posible, y los que prendiere los retendrá en el presidio hasta que disponga el comandante si han de restituirse ó imponérseles alguna pena, prohibiendo todo castigo personal en el campo despues de aprehendidos; y por ningun caso se repartirán los indios arrestados, como indebidamente se ha practicado, antes sí se les tratará y asistirá como está prevenido con los prisioneros de guerra; pero á las mugeres y niños que se cogieren, se les tratará con suavidad, restituirán á sus padres y familias, á fin de que conozcan que no es el encono ni el interés, sino la justa compensacion que promueve las providencias; y esta restitucion se hará ante todos los oficiales que firmarán la entrega, dando cuenta con ella al inspector y este á mi virey.

TITULO ONCE.

Gobierno político.

1. Con los justos fines de que al resguardo de los presidios bien arreglados se fomente la poblacion y comercio en los paises de Frontera, y que igualmente se aumente la fuerza de ellos con el mayor número de habitadores, mando al comandante, capitanes, oficiales y demas personas, no impidan, ni retraigan con pretesto alguno, que las gentes de buena vida y costumbres se avecinden y residan dentro de su recinto; y cuando no bastase este á contener las familias agregadas, se ampliará por alguno de sus lados, haciéndose la obra á cuenta del comun, por redundar en beneficio de todos: y asimismo ordeno á los capitanes, que repartan y señalen tierras y solares, con la obligacion de cultivarlas, á los que las pidieren, y de tener caballo, armas y municiones para salir contra los enemigos cuando lo dicte la necesidad y se les mande, dando la preferencia en el reparto de tierras y solares á los soldados que hubiesen servido los diez años de su empeño, á los que se hubiesen retirado por su ancianidad ó achaques, y á las familias de los que hubiesen fallecido, entregando á unos y otros entonces sus alcances y el fondo de cien pesos que deben tener caidos en caja, para que puedan aviar sus labores.

2. Prohibo espresamente que á los mercaderes de géneros, víveres y otros efectos (que no sean prohibidos), ó á los artistas que quieran ir á trabajar á los presidios, se les moleste, ni impida su establecimiento, venta ó trabajo pasagero; de lo cual será responsable el capitan, como gefe y gobernador de esta poblacion.

lesser excesses, and endeavoring to induce them by good example and persuasion to admit missionaries among them and to submit to my authority; if from time to time (as usual) they steal horses or commit other excesses that cannot be overlooked and on demand they do not make restitution, they will be obliged to do so with force, inflicting the least possible injury on them; those who are captured will be kept in the presidio until the commandant-inspector decides whether they are to make restitution or if some other penalty should be imposed on them, but any bodily punishment in the field after apprehension is prohibited. In no case shall the Indians arrested be sent into servitude as has illegally been done in the past; instead they will be treated and assisted as prescribed for prisoners of war. As for the women and children that are captured, they are to be treated with gentleness, restoring them to their parents and families in order that they recognize that it is not hatred or self-interest but the administration of justice that motivates our laws. This restitution will be made in the presence of all the officers, who will sign the report giving an account of everything to my commandant-inspector, who is to inform my viceroy.

TITLE ELEVEN.

Political Government.

1. With the justified aim that protection by well-regulated presidios will foment settlement and commerce in the frontier area, and that the strength of the presidios likewise will be augmented by a great number of inhabitants, I order the commandant-inspector, captains, officers, and other persons on no pretext to impede or dissuade people of good reputations and habits from entering and settling in their districts; and when their presidio is no longer large enough to contain the incoming families, they are to expand it on one side, the work to be done in common since it redounds to the benefit of all. At the same time I order the captains to distribute and assign lands and town lots to those that ask them, with the obligation that they cultivate them and that they keep horses, arms, and munitions for use in expeditions against enemies when necessity demands it and they are so ordered. In the distribution of lands and town lots, preference will be given to the soldiers who have served their ten-year enlistments and to those who have retired because of old age or illness and to the families of those who have died; to all these will be delivered the balances due them, as well as the one hundred pesos that should have accumulated in the treasury of the common fund, in order that they may provision themselves for their labors.

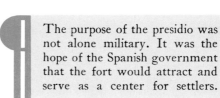

The purpose of the presidio was not alone military. It was the hope of the Spanish government that the fort would attract and serve as a center for settlers.

2. I expressly prohibit the molesting of merchants selling goods, provisions, and other goods (that are not prohibited) or of artisans who wish to work at the presidios, nor are they to be impeded in their establishments, sales, or transient labors; the captain, as chief and governor of the settlement, will be responsible in these matters.

TITULO DOCE.

Funciones del inspector comandante de los presidios internos de Nueva España.

1. El oficial que yo nombrare para este empleo tendrá á lo menos el grado de coronel, y estará inmediata y únicamente (sin intervencion alguna de los inspectores de las tropas del ejército de aquel reino) á las órdenes de mi virey, á quien dará con puntualidad todos los avisos y noticias, asi pertenecientes al estado y fuerzas de los presidios, como por lo que toca á las entradas y operaciones de guerra que proyectare ó hiciere; pero siempre que tenga yo por conveniente verificar la ereccion de una comandancia general de las provincias interiores, estará inmediatamente á las órdenes del oficial general á quien yo tuviese á bien conferirla.

2. El inspector comandante no podrá ser al mismo tiempo gobernador de provincia, ni capitan de presidio, por ser necesario al desempeño de su empleo que siempre esté á la vista de las operaciones y manejo de los gobernadores y capitanes, y variar su residencia, segun lo exija la utilidad de mi servicio.

3. Vigilará que los presidios y compañias de su inspeccion sigan sin variacion alguna todo lo prevenido en este reglamento, para su instruccion, disciplina, servicio, manejo de caudales, interior gobierno, provision &c. Que la subordinacion se observe con vigor; y que desde el capitan, hasta el cabo inclusive, cada uno ejerza y llene las funciones de su empleo: que la tropa reciba puntualmente su prest y raciones; y que en la subministracion de las prendas de armamento, vestuario y montura, como tambien en los efectos que se le diesen para el avio de sus familias, no se la grave ni cargue mas que el costo y costas que hubiesen tenido, procurando que el soldado lo conozca asi: y siendo mi voluntad, que por lo que mira á la subordinacion y leyes penales esté esta tropa en todo lo posible á lo mismo que tengo mandado en las Ordenanzas de mi ejército, cuidará de que las prisiones y demas castigos se arreglen enteramente á lo que previenen: el inspector será responsable de que asi suceda, y para su logro le concedo facultad de reprender, arrestar y suspender en su empleo á cualquiera oficial de los presidios y compañias de su mando; pero en este último caso dará inmediatamente cuenta al virey, con espresion de los motivos, para que resuelva lo que tuviere por conveniente.

4. Revistará anualmente los presidios por sí, ó por alguno de los dos ayudantes que se le destinan, repartiendo con ellos ó entre ellos la Frontera: examinará muy particularmente la conducta y circunstancias de los oficiales, de que informará al virey: cuidará no solo del completo de las compañias, sino mas especialmente de la calidad y aptitud del soldado, del buen estado del armamento, conservacion de la pólvora, destreza del soldado ó indio auxiliar en el manejo de las armas y caballo, y en que se ejerciten con frecuencia en tirar al blanco, objeto muy importante en todas las tropas; pero con especialidad en las de presidios, destinadas á una guerra de distinta naturaleza.

TITLE TWELVE.

Functions of the Commandant-Inspector of the Interior Presidios of New Spain.

1. The officer whom I appoint to this office will be at least of the rank of colonel and will be immediately and solely (without any interference whatsoever by the inspectors of troops of the army in that kingdom) under the orders of my viceroy, to whom he punctually will give all reports and information not only about the status and forces of the presidios but also about all that touches on expeditions and operations of war which he projects or has in progress; but if I find it convenient to establish a commandancy-general for the Interior Provinces, the commandant-inspector immediately will come under the orders of the general officer upon whom I see fit to confer this title.

2. The commandant-inspector will not govern a province at the same time, nor will he be the captain of a presidio, for it is necessary in discharging his duties that he always oversee the operations and management of the governors and captains, and that he change his residence according to the demands and needs of my service.

3. He will be vigilant that the presidios and companies under his control observe without any variation all the requirements of this regulation pertaining to instruction, discipline, duties, management of finances, internal administration, provisioning, etc.; that obedience is vigorously required; and that everyone from captain down to corporal, inclusive, exercise and fulfill the duties of his office. He is to see that the troops punctually receive their pay and rations, and that in the distribution of items of armament, dress, and mounts, as well as in the effects that are given for the upkeep of their families, the soldiers are not burdened or charged more than the cost and expenses of them, working to make the troops understand this. It also is my will that the discipline and penal laws to which the troops are subject be the same, as far as possible, as the ordinances that I have decreed for my army, especially that imprisonments and other punishments conform entirely with these provisions. The commandant-inspector will be responsible in these matters, and in order that he succeed I grant him the authority to reprimand, arrest, or suspend from office any officer in the presidios and companies under his command; but in the latter case he immediately will give an account to the viceroy, with an explanation of his actions, in order that the viceroy may resolve the manner as seems convenient to him.

4. He will hold an annual review of the presidios, either personally or through one of the two assistants that will be assigned to him, dividing the frontier posts with them or between them; he will examine particularly the conduct and reputation of the officers, of which he will inform the viceroy. He will take note not only of the complements of the companies, but more especially of the quality and aptitude of the soldiers, of the good condition of their armament, their conservation of gunpowder, and the dexterity of the soldiers and Indian auxiliaries in the handling of their arms and horses; and that frequent target practice is held, a very important exercise for all troops, but especially in the presidios, which are destined for war of a distinct nature.

The first commandant-general of the Interior Provinces was Don Teodoro de Croix, Caballero of the Teutonic Order, a Frenchman long in the service of the Spanish crown. His uncle had been a viceroy of New Spain.

5. En calidad de **comandante** de los presidios, le concedo facultad para determinar el número, objeto, direccion y tiempos de las patrullas ó destacamentos que hayan de batir la campaña y terrenos intermedios entre unos y otros presidios, como tambien la de reunir estos destacamentos en una ó mas divisiones, para acudir al socorro de algun parage insultado, escarmentar á los bárbaros, ó inquietarlos en sus mismas rancherias, lo que procurará con la frecuencia posible, por tener acreditada la experiencia ser este el medio mas eficaz de contenerlos y alejarlos.

6. Considerando los gastos que se le originarán en los continuos viages para las revistas y reconocimientos, y en las espediciones de guerra, donde juzgare importante su presencia, ó que mandare en persona por órden de mi virey, le concedo el sueldo anual de 8.000 pesos; y mando que se le satisfagan en cualquiera de las cajas señaladas para el pago de situados de presidios de las Provincias Internas.

7. El inspector comandante tendrá privativas facultades en campaña de conceder treguas y suspension de armas á los enemigos cuando la pidieren, y aun de tratar de preliminares de paz; pero siempre expresando á los gefes de ellos, que necesita para ser válida y permanente la confirmacion y aprobacion de mi virey.

8. Cuidará particularmente que todo prisionero ó indio dado de paz sea tratado con humanidad, y asistido con la misma racion que se da á los auxiliares, castigando severamente al oficial, soldado, ú otra persona que indebidamente los maltrate, y sobre todo al que matare alguno á sangre fria.

9. Los dos ayudantes, cuya obligacion es la de aliviarle en el desempeño de su cargo, bajo su direccion y órdenes, tendrán á lo menos el grado de capitan; y por las consideraciones anteriores, concedo á cada uno el sueldo anual de 3 000 pesos, que cobrarán igualmente en cualquiera de dichas cajas.

10. Para la provision de cada uno de estos dos empleos, respecto de ser el inspector comandante responsable de su desempeño, propondrá á mi virey para ahora y en adelante, tres oficiales en quienes concurran las circunstancias de talentos, actividad, celo y espíritu de justicia; pero como sin experimentarse los sugetos no hay precaucion que baste para asegurar el acierto de la eleccion, y es tan importante la de los que han de desempeñar estos empleos, ejerciendo sus funciones á larga distancia del inspector, le ordeno, que antes de proponerlo, se entere bien de sus circunstancias y calidades, y despues vigile su conducta y desempeño, á fin de que si no fuesen á propósito, los separe mi virey de este encargo, dándome parte; y si por lo contrario llenasen bien sus obligaciones, me los recomiende para sus ascensos.

TITULO TRECE.

Funciones y facultades del capitan y demas oficiales, sargentos, cabos, soldados y capellan.

1. La principal obligacion del capitan es observar por sí, y mante-

5. In his capacity as commandant of the presidios, I grant him the authority to determine the number, object, direction, and time of the patrols and detachments sent to scout the countryside and terrain lying between the several presidios, as well as the authority to unite these detachments into one or more divisions to give aid to some threatened place, to punish the barbarians, or to harrass them in their own villages, all of which will be done as frequently as possible, for experience has shown this to be the most effective way to contain them and keep them at a distance.

6. Considering the expenses that will be incurred in continual trips for inspections and reconnaissances and in expeditions of war, on which he deems his presence important or which he commands in person by order of my viceroy, I grant to him an annual salary of 8,000 pesos; and I order that this be paid from any of the treasuries authorized to pay the expenses of the presidios of the Interior Provinces.

7. The commandant-inspector will have special authority in the field of conceding truces and suspensions of fighting to the enemies when they ask for it, and of negotiating the preliminaries of peace; but always he will tell the enemy chieftains that it is necessary for my viceroy to give his confirmation and approval before these become valid and permanent.

8. He will take particular care that all Indian prisoners and those who surrender peacefully be treated with humanity and be provided with the same rations as are given to the auxiliaries; he will castigate severely any officer, soldier, or other person who unnecessarily mistreats them, and most severely those who kill one in cold blood.

9. His two assistants, whose obligation it is to lighten his burdens in the discharge of his office, under his direction and orders will have at least the rank of captain; for the aforementioned considerations, I grant to each one an annual salary of 3,000 pesos, which also may be drawn from any of the aforementioned treasuries.

10. In the filling of each one of these two positions, inasmuch as the commandant-inspector is to be responsible for their performance, he will propose to my viceroy, both now and in the future, three officers in whom are found the characteristics of talent, industry, zeal, and a spirit of justice; but since without examining those suggested, there can be no precaution that they will prove excellent for the office, a position of much importance since it will be performed and its functions exercised at great distances from the commandant-inspector, I order that before recommending them he investigate them closely as to their conduct and qualifications, and afterwards to watch vigilantly their conduct and performance. If they do not prove satisfactory, my viceroy will remove them, notifying me; and if on the other hand they perform their task well, they are to be recommended to me for promotion.

TITLE THIRTEEN.

Duties of the Captain and Other Officers, Sergeants, Corporals, Soldiers, and Chaplain.

1. The principal obligation of the captain is personally to supervise his subordinates and to

ner con firmeza en sus subalternos y tropa la mas exacta observancia de cuanto ordeno en este reglamento y previenen las Ordenanzas generales, en punto á subordinacion y leyes penales, como tambien las órdenes de mi virey y de su inspector comandante; para cuyo efecto le doy la facultad de reprender, arrestar y aun suspender de su empleo en algun caso al oficial subalterno que lo mereciere, dando inmediatamente parte al inspector, y de separar al sargento ó cabo que no observase lo mandado.

2. Siendo mi real ánimo y tan conveniente á mi servicio y al desempeño del mismo capitan que el soldado esté bien asistido, armado y montado, debe vigilar con atencion continua, que los siete caballos y una mula de la dotacion de cada soldado sean del mayor aguante, y propio á la fatiga, revistándolos antes que el soldado los reciba, para ver si son ó no admisibles, y despues en cada mes para desechar los inútiles.

3. Igualmente examinará la calidad de los víveres, prendas de vestuario y montura, á fin de que no se le grave en ella, como ni tampoco en los precios á que se le cargan.

4. Tambien en revistas semanarias inspeccionará el armamento, para que inmediatamente se componga cualquier tornillo ú otra pieza que esté rota ó endeble y cuando el todo de la arma no se halle capáz de admitir una sólida compostura, mandará reemplazarla con una nueva que se cargará al soldado.

5. Pondrá la mayor atencion en los reclutas que admite, teniendo siempre á la vista, que la gente enfermiza ó delicada mas contribuye á la debilidad que á la fuerza de la tropa; y que en unas compañias como la de su mando, destinadas á un servicio de tanta fatiga á marchas rápidas y distantes, y á una guerra en cuyas acciones suele pelearse mas con la fuerza y el valor particular, que con la que infande la union y formacion, no puede dispensarse la mas leve falta en la robustéz, resistencia y resolucion del soldado.

6. A los reclutas dará á su entrada un papel que justifique se ha admitido por tiempo de diez años, y no podrá obligarles á que sirvan mas, á menos de estar en campaña actual; pero tampoco podrá licenciarlos hasta que se pase la revista de inspeccion por el inspector ó alguno de sus ayudantes.

7. Como las ordenanzas de mi ejército señalan las penas para cada falta ó delito en que el soldado incurre, ni dejará de infligirlas, ni podrá agravarlas conviniendo que el soldado conozca que se le castiga con igualdad y justicia.

8. Será precisa obligacion del capitan ejercitar sus soldados en tirar al blanco, en el diestro manejo de sus caballos, y en aquellas evoluciones útiles y adaptables á la especie de guerra que hacen, é inspirar así en ellos, como en los oficiales subalternos, amor á su profesion y á mi servicio, conteniendo y castigando á los que tengan conversaciones que puedan infundir disgusto, siendo mi real ánimo excluir de mi servicio á quien no estuviere contento de su suerte.

maintain firmly among them and the troops the most exact observance of what I have ordered in this regulation and everything prescribed in the general ordinances regarding obedience and penal laws, as well as the orders of my viceroy and of the commandant-inspector; to this end I give him the power to reprimand, arrest, and even suspend from office in any case a subordinate officer who merits it, immediately giving a report to the commandant-inspector; and he can dismiss the sergeant or corporal who does not obey his orders.

2. Since it is my royal will and is so important to my service and to the captain himself in his performance that the soldiers be well provisioned, armed, and mounted, he should be vigilant continually that the seven horses and one mule of the soldier's equipment have the greatest stamina and be able to withstand fatigue; he is to examine them before the soldier receives them in order to see if they are or are not acceptable, and afterward he will examine them once each month in order to discard the unfit.

3. He likewise will examine the quality of the provisions, articles of clothing, and saddles and trappings in order that the soldiers not be imposed upon, and to see that their prices are equitable.

4. Also, in the weekly reviews he will inspect the armament to see that whatever screw or other piece that is broken or about to break is immediately repaired; and when it is not possible to restore the entire weapon to good condition, I order it replaced with a new one, and the soldier will be charged for it.

5. He will give the closest attention to the recruits that he accepts, having always in mind that the sickly or weak person contributes more to weakness than to the strength of the troop; some companies such as the one he commands, are destined to a service of great hardships and to forced marches of great distances, and to a war in which the battles will be fought more with individual strength and valor than with exercises in uniformity and training. He cannot excuse the most minute fault in the health, hardiness, and resolution of a soldier.

6. On their enlistment recruits will be given a paper that certifies that they have been enrolled for a term of ten years and that they will not be obliged to serve more unless they are engaged in an actual campaign; but neither will they be released until they have passed an inspection review by the inspector or one of his assistants.

7. Since the ordinances for my army indicate the penalties that a soldier can incur for each fault or crime, the captain will not neglect to inflict them; but he cannot increase them. Therefore the soldiers will recognize that they will be punished with equality and justice.

8. It will be a specific obligation of the captain to train his soldiers in shooting at targets, in the skillful management of their horses, and in those maneuvers that are useful and adapted to the type of war in which they will be engaged; in this way he will inspire in them and in the subaltern officers a love of their profession and of my service, isolating and punishing those who make conversations that would stir up discontent, for it is my royal pleasure to exclude from my service those who are not content with their lot.

Obligaciones de los oficiales subalternos.

9. Sentada la principal de la subordinacion á sus superiores, y de la exactitud y observancia de cuanto previenen mis Ordenanzas y le manden sus gefes, es tambien de la obligacion de estos oficiales contribuir en cuanto esté de su parte al completo de las del capitan, y en su ausencia cuidar de la compañia que quede á su mando, con la misma responsabilidad y celo; además, deben saber de memoria lo prevenido en este reglamento, y las leyes penales para observarlas y hacerlas cumplir con puntualidad.

Obligaciones del sargento.

10. Debe el sargento saber de memoria todas las obligaciones del soldado y cabo, y las leyes penales para enseñarlas y hacerlas cumplir en su compañia, no disimular cualquier desorden, conversacion prohibida, ó especie que pueda tener trascendencia contra la subordinacion, contener y remediar por sí lo que en el instante pueda, y dar parte despues á su inmediato gefe, haciéndose respetar del soldado por su buena conducta y observancia, y por el respeto y subordinacion que le noten hácia sus oficiales.

Obligacion del cabo.

11. El cabo debe distinguirse de los soldados por su conducta, obediencia y subordinacion á sus gefes, cuidado en la limpieza de sus caballos y armas, exactitud en el servicio, y valor en las ocasiones de guerra para constituirse acreedor á la plaza del sargento y mayores ascensos.

Obligaciones del soldado.

12. El soldado debe tener la mas ciega obediencia y subordinacion á sus cabos, sargentos y oficiales, cuidar de sus caballos, vestuario y armas; enterarse de las penas en que puede incurrir, para evitarlas con su arreglado proceder; procurar distinguirse en las acciones de guerra, y tener una fundada esperanza de mejorar su fortuna.

Funciones y obligaciones del capellan.

13. Es obligacion propia del ministerio de los capellanes, ademas de la administracion de sacramentos, la asistencia y consuelo espiritual de los oficiales y soldados cuando estén enfermos ó heridos; y asimismo la amonestacion suave sobre los defectos de conducta particular en sus casas para con sus mugeres, hijos y familia; y si (precedido un maduro examen) averiguese que alguna persona de la compañia vive escandalosamente, ó introduce mugeres livianas, disfrazada ó públicamente, dará parte al capitan, ó al que en su lugar mandase la compañia, para que aplique el mas pronto remedio, de obviar tales desórdenes,

Duties of subaltern officers.

9. Once the principle of subordination to their superiors and of the exact observance of what is contained in my ordinances and in the orders of their superiors is instilled, it is also the obligation of these officers to contribute in every possible way to help the captain in the completion of his orders; and in his absence they will take charge of the company that is left under their command with the same responsibility and zeal. Moreover, they are to know by memory everything required in this regulation and in the penal laws in order to observe them and to see that they are complied with punctually.

Duties of the sergeant.

10. The sergeant should know from memory all the duties of the soldiers and the corporals, and the penal laws, in order to instruct the company and to see to their compliance. He is not to overlook disorders, prohibited conversations, or incidents that might be contrary to obedience; he personally is to restrain and correct such things as quickly as possible, and to give a report afterward to his immediate superior, winning the respect of the soldiers by his good conduct and obedience and by the respect and obedience he gives to the officers.

Duties of the corporal.

11. The corporal should distinguish himself from the soldiers by his conduct, obedience, and subordination to his superiors, by his care that his horses and arms are kept clean, by his correctness in the service, and by his bravery in time of war; in this manner he will make himself worthy of the billet of sergeant and for higher promotions.

Duties of the soldier.

12. The soldier should give the blindest obedience and subordination to his corporals, sergeants, and officers, should care for his horses, uniforms, and arms, and should acquaint himself with the penalties that he can incur in order to avoid them by his good behavior; he should attempt to distinguish himself in the actions of war, and he should have a fundamental hope of bettering his position.

Functions and duties of the chaplain.

13. It is the proper duty of the chaplain in his ministry, in addition to the administration of the sacraments, to give spiritual aid and counsel to the officers and soldiers that are ill or wounded; also, to admonish them gently for any personal misconduct in their homes with their wives, children, and families; and if (after a judicious inquiry) it is found that some person in the company is living scandalously or bringing in lewd women, secretly or openly, he will inform the captain, or whoever is commanding the company in the captain's place, in order that the promptest remedy can be applied to stop such disorders,

castigando á los culpados segun las circunstancias del caso, y haciendo espeler inmediatamente las tales mugeres, con apercibimiento, de que si volviesen á hallarse culpadas del mismo delito en la compañia ó presidio, se procederá á castigarlas mas severamente.

14. A los vecinos que se agregaren y establecieren en los presidios, ha de administrar el capellan. Y declaro, que mediante el sueldo señalado de cuarenta pesos mensuales, deberá asistir á todos los que componen sus guarniciones, sin llevar derechos algunos, como se observa en el ejército, y bajo las reglas prefinidas en su ordenanza; pues en premio del mérito que hicieren en aquel destino, serán atendidos en la provision de beneficios eclesiásticos, y especialmente en la de capellanías que se hayan de presentar libremente por mi real patronato.

15. Será obligacion de los capellanes tener un libro de registro, á manera y con la misma formalidad que el que tienen los párrocos territoriales, en que harán su asiento de las partidas de los bautizados, confirmados, casados, difuntos y estado de almas de la tropa, y otro separado de los vecinos agregados al presidio.

16. Siempre que muera un soldado, de cuya cuenta resulte alcance á su favor, y no hubiere hecho disposicion alguna, ni declarados herederos, se solicitará saber si los tiene, y en caso de no encontrarse, se dispondrá de él con intervencion y conocimiento del capitan, á beneficio de su alma, correspondiendo en este caso las tres partes del alcance al capellan, y la cuarta se dará de limosna.

17. Los capellanes deben salir á campaña siempre que se les prevenga por los capitanes, ó el comandante inspector, quien vigilará que en esto no haya exceso, ni otro objeto que el verdadero de mi servicio.

TITULO CATORCE.

Obligaciones y nombramiento del habilitado.

1. La primera obligacion del oficial habilitado es la de corresponder á la confianza que de él hace su compañia, fiandole el manejo de sus intereses, procediendo en él con la limpieza y honor inseparables de su profesion, y procurando (sin detrimento de la calidad de los efectos) la posible baratura en los precios de su primera compra y gastos de su conduccion, como que de esta atencion resulta el bien de todos, y la opinion que formarán de su equidad y celo.

2. Llevará las cuentas generales de cargo y data con la mayor claridad y justificacion, para que al cabo del año examinadas y aprobadas por el capitan y demás oficiales, lo sean tambien por el inspector.

3. Tambien llevará con las mismas circunstancias la cuenta particular de cada individuo, y se enterará con frecuencia de las de los soldados, para advertir á los que por desgracia, enfermedades ó desperdicios se hallen con cortos ó ningunos alcances, que en las listas de lo que pidieren se les traiga al tiempo de enviar por los situados, se ciñan á lo absolutamente necesario; y si continuasen en su poco arreglo, dará cuenta al capitan, para que mande se le retenga parte de los dos reales diarios que se le han de subministrar en dinero.

punishing the guilty according to the circumstances of the case and expelling the women immediately with a warning that if they return and again are found guilty of the same offense in the company or presidio they will be prosecuted and most severely punished.

14. The chaplain will also minister to the civilians who attach themselves to and live in the presidios. And I declare that, because of his stipulated monthly salary of forty pesos, he must attend to all those in the garrison without any additional fees whatsoever, as is the procedure in the army and under the rules stipulated in its ordinances; as a reward for the merit that they show in this office, chaplains will be remembered in the assignment of ecclesiastical benefits, especially in that of the chaplaincies that can be liberally distributed under my royal patronage.

15. It will be the duty of the chaplains to keep a registry book in the manner and with the same formality that is followed by the priests in territorial parishes; in this registry they will keep a record of the persons that are baptized, confirmed, married, died, and the state of the souls of the troops; a separate book will be kept for the civilians who attach themselves to the presidio.

16. Always upon the death of a soldier, in whose account there is a balance in his favor and who has made no disposition for it and who has no acknowledged heirs, efforts will be made to discover if he has any heirs; in case they are not found, the money will be expended with the supervision and knowledge of the captain for the benefit of the dead soldier's soul, corresponding in such cases to three-quarters to be turned over to the chaplain and one-quarter to be given as alms.

17. Chaplains always will go on campaigns when bidden to do so by the captains or by the commandant-inspector, who will be vigilant that in this there are no excesses or any other object than the good of my service.

TITLE FOURTEEN.

Duties and selection of the paymaster.

1. The first obligation of the paymaster is to be worthy of the confidence placed in him by the company in the management of its interests, proceeding in his assignment with the integrity and honor inseparable from his profession, and procuring the goods (without detriment to the quality) at the lowest possible prices both for the initial cost and for the expenses of transportation. Such attention will result to the common good and affect the opinion that the soldiers form as to his honesty and zeal.

2. He will keep the general accounts of debits and credits with the greatest clarity and justification in order that at the end of the year they can be examined and approved by the captain and other officers, as well as by the inspector.

3. He also will keep in a similar manner the particular account of each individual, and will examine frequently those of the soldiers in order that those who through misfortune, sickness, or improvidence have small balances or none at all can be warned to restrict themselves to absolute necessities when the time comes for them to order their allotments; and if such individuals continue their heedless ways, he will give an account of it to the captain so that he can order the withholding of part of the two reales daily that is paid in cash.

The church continued to benefit under the Spanish Bourbon kings, although not to the extent it had prior to 1700 when the throne was held by the Hapsburgs.

4. Deberá tener el suficiente repuesto de víveres para la subministracion de raciones, y para habilitar la tropa en las salidas y espediciones, y otro de todas las prendas de vestuario y montura que usa el soldado, para irle subministrando las que prevenga el capitan, de resultas de las revistas de ropa que deben pasarse cada semana.

5. Será conveniente que siempre que falleciese algun soldado, y sus herederos quieran vender los caballos y armamento del difunto, los compre el habilitado para aviar al recluta que lo reemplace, á quien no podrán cargársele á mas precio que al que las tomó.

6. Lo mismo se practicará con las referidas prendas y caballerías que tomase el fondo (precedida tasacion) para reintegrarse en caso de deuda del difunto, cumplido ó licenciado.

7. Prohibo espresamente al oficial habilitado, que por ningun caso ni pretesto pueda cargar al soldado en las subministraciones que les haga de víveres, vestuario y demás efectos, mas que el coste y costas que tuvieren, pena de privacion de empleo, y de no poder obtener otro en mi servicio. Y si incurriese en quiebra culpable ó estravio de caudales, se le impondrá la misma, y además la prision en un castillo hasta que satisfaga.

8. El habilitado hará al capitan, oficiales, capellan, sargento y soldados el descuento de dos por ciento por las agencias y gastos que le ocasiona su comision.

9. Siempre que hubiere de nombrarse habilitado, prevendrá el capitan á los cabos y soldados de su compañia, que se junten en la habitacion del sargento, para nombrar un apoderado, que puede serlo el mismo sargento, alguno de los cabos ó de ellos mismos; y participado á su capitan el nombramiento, convocará éste con la brevedad posible en su casa á los oficiales subalternos, al capellan y á la persona que hubiere apoderado su compañia, para nombrar á uno de los dichos oficiales subalternos, y no otro por habilitado de ella.

10. Si de los cinco votos hubiese dos por uno, y tres por el otro, habrán de conformarse los dos que fueron de contrario dictamen, y constituirse responsables como si hubiesen votado á su favor; y si en los presidios donde hay tres subalternos resultasen tres votos á favor de cada uno de los dos, ó dos votos á favor de cada uno de los tres, decidirá interinamente el capitan hasta que lo apruebe el inspector.

11. Luego que esté formalizada la eleccion, se estenderá el nombramiento y poder, el cual presentado en la caja correspondiente donde se haya de percibir el situado, servirá de documento y fianza, para la responsabilidad de los caudales.

12. Cada tres años se procederá de nuevo á la nominacion de oficial habilitado, bien para reelegir el actual, ó para nombrar otro; y como en el corto número de dos ó tres oficiales subalternos, que tiene cada presidio, puede encontrarse que ninguno es á propósito para encargo, en que no basta la legalidad sin el genio é inteligencia, podrá el inspector en este caso consultarlo al virey, para con su aprobacion verificar la permuta con otro de presidio ó regimiento capáz de desempeñarlo.

13. Todo lo que no esté prevenido en el presente reglamento, y no

4. He must have a sufficient store of provisions on hand for the distribution of rations and for supplying the troops on their sorties and expeditions, and also all the items of uniforms and equipment used by the soldiers in order to issue it as ordered by the captain after the clothing inspections that are held each week.

5. It will be advisable that always when some soldier dies and his heirs wish to sell his horses and armament the paymaster should buy these in order to supply the recruit who replaces the deceased, but the recruit will not be charged a higher price for them than the one at which they were taken in.

6. The same will be practiced with the aforementioned goods and horses acquired by the common fund (after appraisal) for repayment of the debt of a deceased, retired, or released soldier.

7. I expressly forbid the official paymaster in any case or under any circumstances from charging more than the cost and expenses to the soldiers in the issues that he makes of supplies, clothing, and other effects, on pain of deprivation of office and of never being able to hold another in my service. And if he should become involved in culpable bankruptcy or financial loss, the same penalty will be imposed, and, moreover, he will be confined in a prison until he makes restitution.

8. The paymaster will collect from the captain, officers, chaplain, sergeants, and soldiers a commission of two per cent for the services and expenses that are occasioned by his office.

9. Always when a paymaster is to be named, the captain will summon the corporals and soldiers of his company to assemble in the quarters of the sergeant and name a representative, who may be the sergeant himself, one of the corporals, or one of the privates; after they make known their choice to the captain, he will convoke in his quarters as soon as possible the subaltern officers, the chaplain, and the representative of the company in order to name one of the said subaltern officers, and no other, as paymaster for the company.

10. If of the five votes two are cast for one officer and three for the other, the two who are in the minority will accept the majority will and consider themselves as responsible for his choice as if they had voted for him; and if in the presidios where there are three subaltern officers it happens that three votes are cast for each of two of them, or two votes are cast in favor of each of the three, the captain will make an interim decision until his choice is approved by the commandant-inspector.

11. When the election is made official, the appointment and authority of the paymaster will be documented; when presented to the corresponding treasury where the company receives its allowances, his papers will serve as a record and a bond for the responsibility of the funds.

12. Every three years each company will proceed again to name an official paymaster, either re-electing the incumbent or naming another one; as each presidio has only the small number of two or three subaltern officers, it may be found that none of them is suited to this office, and legality alone, without ability and intelligence, are not sufficient. In this case the commandant-inspector will consult with the viceroy in order that with his approval he can arrange an exchange with another presidio for an officer capable of the discharge of these duties.

13. All that is not included in the present regulation, and

The frugal nature of the king is revealed. It cost the crown nothing to operate a paymaster system in the provincial army.

sea perteneciente á subordinacion y leyes penales, lo determinará mi virey; y cuanto en este particular observare el inspector comandante, se lo hará presente, para que determine lo que tuviere por mas conveniente á mi servicio. Y si algun punto de este reglamento encontrase en la práctica inconveniente grave. Concedo facultad a mi virey para que providencie interinamente, dándome parte de los motivos, para mi resolucion.

Instruccion para la nueva colocacion de presidios.

1. No siendo suficiente para el importante objeto de la pacificacion y seguridad de las provincias internas de nueva España, que las compañias presidiales se pongan sobre el mas ventajoso pie, si su colocacion por defectuosa dificulta el mutuo socorro de unos presidios á otros, y la proporcion de batir la campaña intermedia, he determinado, que la linea de Frontera la formen los quince presidios del Altar, Tubac, Terrenate, Fronteras, Janos, San Buenaventura, Paso del Norte, Guajoquilla, Julimes, Cerro gordo, San Sabá, Santa Rosa, Monclova, San Juan Bautista, y el de la Bahía del Espíritu Santo, segun demuestra el mapa que formó el ingeniero ordinario D. Nicolás Lafora; como tambien que los once que se trasplantan, el de Janos, y los puertos de Robledo y Arroyo del Cíbolo, que han de guardarse con destacamentos de los presidios de Santa Fé y San Antonio de Bejar, aseguren sus recintos, construyéndolos segun el plan del mismo ingeniero. Y ordeno á mi virey, que con la brevedad posible, y precedidos los exámenes, que mandará hacer por personas inteligentes, de los terrenos despejados, y abundantes de aguas y pastos, que no difieran mucho de los parages indicados en dicho mapa, ni de la distancia de cuarenta leguas, en que con corta variacion deben situarse unos de otros, no omita precaucion gasto, ni providencia de cuantas conduzcan á la pronta formacion del cordon de Frontera, y á lo demás que para la seguridad de esta se contiene en la instruccion siguiente.

CORDON DE PRESIDIOS.

Altar.

2. Es el primero de los fronterizos el presidio de Altar, que hallándose actualmente situado á 30 leguas de Vizani y Pitiqui, pueblos pertenecientes á la antigua mision de Caborca, destruida por los Apaches, se debe remover y colocar en otro parage mas inmediato á la Costa del Golfo de Californias, procurando establecerlo en terreno llano donde haya agua y pastos suficientes para la caballada, y en que no sea dificil á sus destacamentos recorrer y batir los distritos que han de quedar por derecha é izquierda desde este presidio á las orillas del mar, y al inmediato de la línea, para impedir que los enemigos del rumbo del Norueste se internen á hostilizar la provincia.

does not pertain to subordination and penal laws, will be determined by my viceroy; anything of this nature which the commandant-inspector observes is to be referred to the viceroy for him to decide it as he thinks best for the betterment of my service. And if any point in this regulation is found in its application to be gravely inadvisable, I concede the authority to my viceroy to change it temporarily, giving me a report of his reason for my deposition.

Instructions for the new location of presidios.

1. It is not sufficient for the important purpose of the pacification and security of the Interior Provinces of New Spain that the presidial companies be put on the most advantageous footing if the location of the presidios is so poor as to make it difficult for them to give mutual aid to one another and to recoinnoiter the intervening terrain; I have determined that the line of the frontier is to be formed of the fifteen presidios of Altar, Tubac, Terrenate, Fronteras, Janos, San Buenaventura, Paso del Norte, Guajoquilla, Julimes, Cerro Gordo, San Sabá, Santa Rosa, Monclova, San Juan Bautista, and that of La Bahía del Espíritu Santo, as shown on the map drawn up by the engineer-in-ordinary Don Nicolás Lafora; also besides the eleven that are to be moved, that of Janos and the outposts of Robledo and Arroyo del Cíbolo are to be guarded by detachments from the presidios of Santa Fé and San Antonio de Béjar and their enclosures strengthened, constructing them according to the plan of the same engineer. And I order my viceroy as quickly as possible, after a careful examination which he will order made by intelligent persons of cleared lands with an abundance of water and pasture, to build presidios at those locations which will not vary much from the sites indicated on the said map and are approximately forty leagues apart one from another. No precaution, expense, or provision conducive to the prompt formation of the cordon of the frontier is to be omitted, or anything else pertaining to its security, as indicated by the following instruction.

See Appendix A for additional information on these presidios. The map opposite page 80 shows the presidial cordon in 1780.

CORDON OF PRESIDIOS.

Altar.

2. The first of the frontier presidios is Altar, which at present actually is situated 30 leagues from Vizani and Pitiqui, towns attached to the old mission of Caborca, which was destroyed by the Apaches; this presidio should be removed and relocated at another site closer to the coast of the Gulf of California, trying to establish it on level terrain where adequate water and fodder are found for the horses and where it will not be difficult for its detachments to survey and reconnoiter the areas which are to the right and left between the presidio and the edge of the sea and between it and the next presidio in the line, in order to prevent the enemies from the northwest from intruding and raiding in the province.

Tubac.

3. A menos distancia de 40 leguas del anterior presidio se halla el de Tubac, con un competente vecindario, que se ha congregado á la sombra de su guarnicion, y los vecinos pueden subsistir en aquel parage, trasladándose la compañia á otro de sus cercanías, donde ofrezca el terreno las proporciones indispensables, y la de situarse precisamente á la misma distancia de 40 leguas de Altar, acercándose á este fin cuanto sea posible hácia el Oeste, con el objeto de asegurar su recíproca comunicacion, cortar promiscuamente rastros en el terreno intermedio, y embarazar las entradas de los enemigos del pais interior.

Terrenate.

4. Se halla establecido este presidio en menos distancia de Tubac de las 40 leguas, que á corta diferencia han de tener entre sí todos los de la línea, y por lo mismo debe removerse y situarse, precediendo individual reconocimiento de los terrenos, en alguno de los muchos valles que bañan los rios de San Pedro, las Nutrias, Guachuca, Terrenate y otros, procurando dejar casi á su espalda las Sierras de Magallanes y Mababe, y en mas cercanía al presidio de Fronteras, para que asi puedan impedir las invasiones de los Apaches, y auxiliarse mutuamente sus destacamentos de los dos colaterales.

Fronteras.

5. Respecto de hallarse tan mal situado este presidio, en que hay un mediano vecindario, que dista 60 leguas del de Janos, dejando por consiguiente descubierta una gran parte de la Frontera mas espuesta á las incursiones de los Apaches Jileños, se ha de trasladar con la posible brevedad al valle de San Bernardino, ú otro parage inmediato, si lo hubiese mas ventajoso, con el preciso destino, de que cruzándose y uniéndose sus destacamentos con los de Janos y Terrenate, contengan las entradas de aquellos bárbaros, cayéndoles con frecuencia sobre sus cercanos aduares ó rancherías.

6. Los sitios en que actualmente se hallan los referidos cuatro presidios de la Frontera de Sonora han de quedar á la traslacion de ellos, ocupados con el vecindario que tuvieren, y además se deberán agregar otros pobladores españoles, é indios Opatas, dándose á todos repartimiento de tierras y casas ó solares para fabricarlas, con las precisas condiciones de mantenerse equipados y dispuestos á defender sus respectivos distritos, y auxiliar los destacamentos de la tropa que han de resguardar la Frontera; á cuyo fin se proveerá á los españoles de las armas que necesiten por el mero costo que tuvieren á mi real hacienda; y á dichos indios Opatas se les darán de cuenta de ella escopetas, ó carabinas, por su notorio valor, y la constante fidelidad que tienen acreditada desde que voluntariamente entraron en mi dominio.

Tubac.

3. At a distance of less than 40 leagues from the aforementioned presidio is found that of Tubac, with a considerable number of civilians in the vicinity who have congregated there in the shadow of its garrison; the civilians can subsist in that place even if the company is transferred to another site nearby where the terrain offers the indispensible requirements and which is situated precisely the exact distance of forty leagues from Altar, keeping as far as possible to the west with the object of assuring reciprocal communication, cutting indiscriminate paths through the intervening terrain, and hindering the raids of the enemies to the interior country.

The State of Arizona has established the Tubac Presidio Historical Monument and a museum on the site of the old presidio of Tubac.

Terrenate.

4. This presidio was established at less distance from Tubac than the 40 leagues that all presidios of the line are to have, more or less, between one another, and for this reason should be removed and situated, following an individual reconnaissance of the terrain, in one of the many valleys bathed by the rivers San Pedro, Las Nutrias, Guachuta, Terrenate, and others, trying to locate it with the mountain ranges of Magallanes and Mababe almost at their shoulders, and closer to the presidio of Fronteras in order that it can impede the invasions of the Apaches and that these two presidios can render mutual assistance to one another.

Fronteras.

5. This presidio, at which there is a medium-sized group of civilians, finds itself very badly situated, and 60 leagues from Janos, consequently leaving uncovered a large part of the frontier, that part most exposed to the incursions of the Gileño Apaches; it is to be transferred with the greatest brevity to the valley of San Bernardino, or some adjacent site if a more advantageous one can be found, with the precise purpose of alternating and combining its detachments with those of Janos and Terrenate in order to contain the penetrations of the barbarians, frequently raiding their nearby settlements or *rancherías*.

6. The sites in which the above-mentioned four presidios of the frontier of Sonora now stand, when the presidios are removed, are to remain occupied by the civilians now there, and moreover other Spanish settlers or Ópata Indians should be moved there, giving to all a distribution of land and houses, or town lots on which to build them; the only specific condition to be made is that they keep themselves equipped and disposed to defend their respective districts and to help the detachments of troops that are guarding the frontier. To this end the Spaniards will be sold the necessary arms at their exact cost to my royal treasury; and the said Ópata Indians will be given muskets or carbines because of their well-known valor, and because of the constant fidelity which they have manifested since they voluntarily entered my dominion.

Janos.

7. Este presidio, que es de los mas importantes y su posicion muy oportuna á cortar el paso á los Apaches Jileños que infestan la Sonora y Nueva Vizcaya, debe quedar en el valle donde está arreglando su antigua construccion al nuevo plan que se ha formado para todos los presidios; y auxiliada esta compañia recíprocamente de las partidas de sus dos colindantes de Fronteras y San Buenaventura, que tambien se debe mudar, cuidará de oponerse constantemente á las invasiones de los bárbaros.

8. No obstante de que este presidio corresponde á la Provincia de la Nueva Vizcaya, conviene por su inmediacion á las sierras y fronteras de Sonora, que los diez indios exploradores de su compañia sean de la nacion de los Opatas, como lo han de ser los de Fronteras, Tubac, Terrenate, y el Altar, y que en las ocasiones de salidas contra los Jilenos se franquee al capitan de Janos de las inmediatas misiones de la Sierra los demás indios auxiliares que pida y necesite, sin impedirles que puedan voluntariamente establecerse al abrigo del mismo presidio, ó en los parages cercanos al de Casas Grandes, hacienda de Becerra y otros muy fértiles, que antes estuvieron poblados, y que son bien oportunos á cerrar el paso de la Frontera por aquella parte.

San Buenaventura.

9. Los recomendables objetos que se tuvieron presentes para convenir en la ereccion de este presidio, se malograron todos con haberlo establecido en el valle de San Buenaventura, situado en la profundidad que forman la inaccesible sierra de San Miguel y el Cerro Alto, y de consiguiente espuesto á una multitud de avenidas y gargantas encubiertas, por las cuales le combaten de continuo los enemigos; y para remediar semejantes daños y otros muchos que resultan de su mala posicion, mando: que cuanto antes sea posible, se mude, reteniendo su propio nombre, al valle de Ruiz, construyéndolo en la cercanía de la laguna de Guzman, á fin de que hallándose en casi igual altura que el de Janos, y en la distancia señalada de 40 leguas, quede puesto en la línea de Frontera, y puedan sus destacamentos resguardar el distrito de ella, con el auxilio de sus dos colindantes por derecha é izquierda.

Paso del Norte.

10. Al abrigo de este antiguo presidio se halla establecido el numeroso pueblo de su nombre, que con las misiones inmediatas cuenta mas de cinco mil personas; y bien armados sus vecinos, pueden y deben defenderse por sí mismos, cumpliendo con la obligacion contraida en su establecimiento, y las condiciones impuestas en la reparticion de los fértiles terrenos que ocupan, por cuyos motivos y el de continuar el cordon de Frontera, mando: que esta compañia pase sin pérdida de tiempo á establecer el presidio en las inmediaciones del pueblo del Car-

Janos.

7. This presidio, which is of the most importance and whose position is very opportune to cut the passage of the Gileño Apaches that infest Sonora and Nueva Vizcaya, should remain in the valley where it now is, arranging its old buildings to the new plan that has been formed for all the presidios; this company, reciprocally aiding the parties from the two contiguous presidios of Fronteras and San Buenaventura, which are to be moved, will constantly take care to oppose the invasions of the barbarians.

8. Notwithstanding that this presidio is attached to the province of Nueva Vizcaya, it is desirable, because of its proximity to the mountains and frontiers of Sonora, that the ten Indian scouts of its company be of the Ópata nation, as will be those of Fronteras, Tubac, Terrenate, and Altar; and on the occasions of expeditions against the Gileños, the captain at Janos is to requisition from the nearby mountain missions as many Indian auxiliaries as he wants and needs. These Indians are not to be impeded from voluntarily establishing themselves in the shelter of the said presidio or in places close to Casas Grandes, the Becerra hacienda, or other very fertile places which earlier were populated and which are very opportune to block the pass along that part of the frontier.

San Buenaventura.

9. The commendable objectives that were borne in mind at the erection of this presidio completely miscarried because it was established in the valley of San Buenaventura, which is a deep valley formed by the inaccessible mountain ranges of San Miguel and Cerro Alto; as a consequence it is exposed to a multitude of avenues and hidden gorges through which enemies continue to move to attack it. In order to remedy such assaults and many other dangers that result from its poor location, I order that as soon as possible it be moved, retaining its present name, to the Ruiz Valley and constructed in the vicinity of Lake Guzman, so that it is situated in almost equal latitude as that of Janos and at the appointed distance of 40 leagues from it; it will remain in the line of the frontier, and its detachments can guard its district with the aid of the two adjoining presidios to its right and left.

Paso del Norte.

10. In the protection of this old presidio a populous town of the same name has been established which, with the nearby missions, numbers more than five thousand persons; since the inhabitants are well armed, they can and should defend themselves by themselves, thus complying with the obligation contracted at the establishment of the town and the conditions imposed in the distribution of the fertile lands which they occupy. For this reason and in order to continue the cordon of the frontier, I order that this company without loss of time move to establish a presidio in the vicinity of the town of

The presidio was located on the west bank of the Rio Grande, within the area encompassed by the present Mexican city of Juarez, Chihuahua, across the river from modern El Paso, Texas.

[53]

rizal, y en el parage espacioso y llano que se reconociere ser mas abundante de agua y pastos, con la mira de que situado en la línea y distancia proyectadas con el de San Buenaventura, puedan ambos darse la mano y cruzarse sus destacamentos, resguardando de este modo la provincia, y especialmente la villa de Chihuahua.

11. Con el fin de mantener la libre comunicacion con la provincia de la Nueva México, y de proveer á la seguridad del pueblo del Paso y sus cercanas misiones de indios, se destinará desde luego por mi virey un oficial subalterno del ejército, de acreditada conducta, con el sueldo de mil pesos, para que en calidad de teniente gobernador arregle en compañias formales de milicias el vecindario del Paso, compuesto de españoles y otras clases de gentes, á quienes se proveerá de las armas necesarias por el costo que hubieren tenido a mi real hacienda, con la mira de que atiendan a su propia defensa, y escolten el cordon de arrieros y pasageros que anualmente suben y bajan de la Nueva México, hasta el parage nombrado de Robledo, distante veinte leguas, donde se ha de establecer un destacamento y nuevo pueblo por el gobierno de aquella provincia, como se prevendra en su lugar.

Guajoquilla.

12. Desde el parage del Carrizál, en que ha de establecerse el anterior presidio del Paso, y a la distancia aprobada de cuarenta leguas a corta diferiencia, debe situarse otro de los que existen internados en la Nueva Vizcaya, y sera el de Guajoquilla, trasladandolo con la posible prontitud, al Valle de S. Eleceario, donde continuando la línea de Frontera hasta cerca de las orillas del rio grande del Norte, podrán sus partidas impedir las continuas entradas que hacen los enemigos por los puertos y gargantas de la Cueva, el Nogal, Peña Blanca y otras por donde se internan hasta el camino real que baja de Chihuahua á Durango.

Julimes.

13. Este presidio que se halla tambien internado sobre el rio de Conchos, estaba ventajosamente situado en la junta de éste y el del Norte, donde su utilísima ereccion costó grandes dificultades, y por una precipitada providencia se mudó al parage donde subsiste; y debiendo proveer de remedio á los graves daños que se han originado de aquella perjudicial novedad en el abandono de seis pueblos de indios norteños, que de consiguiente se destruyeron, y en haber dejado franco el paso á los enemigos que luego ocuparon y demolieron una gran parte de la fábrica del antiguo presidio. Mando, que sin retardacion y con todos los auxilios que éste necesite de los inmediatos, se restituya su compañia al mismo parage de la junta, procurando el capitan al propio tiempo reunir los espresados indios norteños, que son de acreditado valor á sus pueblos desiertos, con el fin de cerrar aquel paso á los Notagés y demás bárbaros que habitan á la vanda opuesta del rio del Norte.

Carrizal, and on a spacious and level site which upon inspection proves to be very abundant in water and pasture; as a result of this move it will be situated in the line at the projected distance from San Buenaventura; they can give each other a hand and interchange their detachments, in this way protecting the province and especially the villa of Chihuahua.

11. With the view of maintaining free communication with the province of New Mexico and of providing security to the town of El Paso and its nearby missions and mission Indians, my viceroy will appoint at once a subaltern army officer of good conduct, at a salary of one thousand pesos, who in the capacity of lieutenant governor will organize the civilians at El Paso, composed of Spaniards and other persons, into regular companies of militia; they will be provided with the necessary arms at the cost at which they were acquired by my royal treasury, so that they can attend to their own defense and can escort to Robledo, twenty leagues distant, the trains of muleteers and travelers who annually go to and from New Mexico. At that point will be established a detachment and new town by the governor of that province, as will be provided for in its proper place.

Guajoquilla.

12. From the district of Carrizal, at which will be established the abovementioned presidio of El Paso, and at the approved distance of about forty leagues, will be located another of the presidios which are in the interior of Nueva Vizcaya, that of Guajoquilla, removing it with the greatest promptness to the Valley of San Eleazario; from this new site, which will continue the line of the frontier almost to the banks of the Rio Grande, parties will be able to impede the continuous raids which the enemies make by way of the passes and gorges of La Cueva, El Nogal, Peña Blanca, and others through which they penetrate to the *camino real* that runs from Chihuahua to Durango.

Julimes.

13. This presidio, which is also in the interior on the Conchos River, was advantageously situated at the junction of this river and the Del Norte, where it was erected with great difficulties; then by a hasty decision it was moved to the place where it now stands. There should be provided a remedy for the grave damages that originated in that prejudicial innovation, whereby six villages of northern Indians were abandoned and subsequently were destroyed, as a result leaving open a path to the enemy, who immediately occupied the area and demolished a large part of the buildings of the old presidio. I order that without delay and with all the help necessary from the presidios in the vicinity the company be returned to the original site at the junction of the rivers, the captain endeavoring at the same time to reunite at their deserted villages the aforesaid northern Indians, whose valor is wellknown. In this way the pass used by the Natages and other barbarians that inhabit the opposite bank of the Rio Grande can be closed.

Cerro Gordo, San Sabá, Santa Rosa, Monclova.

14. Como la mejor barrera que pueden tener las provincias de Nueva Vizcaya y Coahuila, desde el presidio de la Junta hasta el de San Juan Bautista, es el Rio Grande del Norte, cuyo curso de un punto á otro de los dos citados presidios, se regula á juicio prudente de ciento cuarenta leguas de distancia, y con la justa idea de cubrir ventajosamente la frontera de ambas provincias, aprovechando las buenas proporciones que franquea el mismo rio del Norte intransitable por muchos parages, se deberán situar con inmediacion á sus orillas y en todo el claro que hay entre dichos presidios de la Junta y San Juan Bautista, los cuatro nombrados el Cerro Gordo, San Sabá, Santa Rosa y Monclova, que al presente son inútiles y aun muy perjudicial el segundo en los parages donde existen, por dejar franca entrada á la multitud de enemigos que inundan, talan y roban hasta lo interior de la Vizcaya, sin que se liberte de sus piraterías y estragos la gobernacion de Coahuila.

15. Deben reconocerse con proligidad los terrenos que median entre los dos citados presidios de la Junta y San Juan Bautista, por el actual comandante de la Frontera de la Nueva Vizcaya y el gobernador de Coahuila, en virtud de las instrucciones y órdenes que á este intento tenga dadas mi virey; y para que lo ejecuten cada uno por su parte, con presencia de todos los documentos conducentes, y que puedan ir estableciendo succesivamente y en proporcionadas distancias los cuatro presidios que han de trasladarse sobre las orillas del rio del Norte en parages llanos y fértiles, se les remitirán cópias del informe y dictámenes del marqués de Rubí, con el mapa de la Frontera, formado por el ingeniero D. Nicolás Lafora, y de los derroteros de D. Pedro de Rávago y Terán, gobernador que fué de Coahuila, encargándoles, que procuren adquirir los que formó el partidario Berroterán, capitan de presidio de Conchos, que se podrán tal vez hallar en poder de sus herederos.

16. A efecto de conseguir con la brevedad posible el objeto de cerrar aquella frontera, situando los referidos cuatro presidios á iguales y proporcionadas distancias sobre las márgenes del rio del Norte, ordeno á los dichos comandante de la Nueva Vizcaya y gobernador de Coahuila, que separadamente y á un mismo tiempo procedan á ejecutar el reconocimiento de los terrenos, tomando el primero la tropa necesaria y las compañias de Julimes, Cerro Gordo y San Sabá, para que restituida la primera á su antiguo presidio de la Junta, se establezca la segunda en el que de nuevo se debe erigir siguiendo el curso del citado Rio Grande; y uniendo el segundo las dos de Santa Rosa y Monclova, explore el país que media entre el presidio de San Juan Bautista y el confluente que forman el rio de San Diego y el del Norte, y erija con ellas los dos nuevos presidios, el uno que resguarde la villa de San Fernando de Austria, dejándola á su espalda, y el otro inmediato á la desembocadura del espresado rio de San Diego; y despues resuelvan de acuerdo el sitio en que deba ponerse el presidio de

Cerro Gordo, San Sabá, Santa Rosa, and Monclova.

14. The best barrier that can be had for the provinces of Nueva Vizcaya and Coahuila—that is, from the presidio of La Junta to that of San Juan Bautista—is the Rio Grande del Norte, whose course from the one point to the other by prudent estimate is 140 leagues in distance. With the sound idea of protecting advantageously the frontier of both provinces, taking advantage of the excellent opportunities offered by the said Rio del Norte, which is impassable at many places, the four presidios named El Cerro Gordo, San Sabá, Santa Rosa, and Monclova should be situated close to its banks at open places that are between the said presidios of La Junta and San Juan Bautista. At present these four are useless, the second-named very harmful, at the places where they are located, for they allow easy entry to the multitude of enemies that overrun, desolate, and rob as far as the interior of Nueva Vizcaya, not leaving the province of Coahuila free from their piracies and ravages.

15. The terrain between the two presidios of La Junta and San Juan Bautista should be recoinnoitered scrupulously by the present commandant of the frontier of Nueva Vizcaya and the governor of Coahuila in accordance with the instructions and orders given them to this effect by my viceroy; there will be remitted to each of these captains copies of the report and findings of the Marqués de Rubí, together with the map of the frontier prepared by the engineer Don Nicolás Lafora and the route charts of Don Pedro Rávago y Terán, the former governor of Coahuila, in order that each captain on his part can execute these orders, with the appropriate documents in hand, and successively re-establish at the proportionate distance and at level and fertile places the four presidios which are to be moved to the banks of the Rio del Norte. The captains are also to be instructed to attempt to procure the charts made by the partisan Berroterán, captain of the presidio of Conchos, which they perhaps can find in the possession of his heirs.

16. To effect as soon as possible the object of closing the said frontier by locating the aforesaid four presidios at equal and proportionate distances along the banks of the Rio del Norte, I order the said commandant of Nueva Vizcaya and the governor of Coahuila separately but at the same time to proceed to execute a reconnaissance of the area; the commandant is to take the necessary troops and the companies from Julimes, Cerro Gordo, and San Sabá in order that with the first of the three restored to its old presidio of La Junta, the second can be located in a new presidio to be erected along the course of the said Rio Grande. The governor will unite the two companies of Santa Rosa and Monclova, explore the country that intervenes between the presidio of San Bautista and the confluence of the rivers San Diego and the Del Norte; with these two companies he will erect two new presidios, one to guard the villa of San Fernando de Austria to its back and the other to be located near the mouth of the San Diego River. Afterward the commandant and governor will agree upon the site where the presidio of San Sabá should be placed, whose company has been withdrawn pending relocation of the mission of El Cañon, where it has been, to the said villa of San Fernando.

Captain Pedro de Rábago y Terán governed Coahuila between 1744 and 1754. He died in Texas early in 1756.

Just as the Spaniards came to the Southwest with fixed ideas about how to wage war, and were forced by circumstances to change, so also the American troops who came to this region in the 1850's brought with them preconceived notions of fighting. Trained in the East and accustomed to fighting Indians with fixed abodes and a forest culture, American officers approached the plains country attempting to meet the Indian menace with infantry. The folly of pursuing mounted Apaches with foot soldiers was continued for almost ten years. Not until post-Civil War years did the U. S. Army really make full use of cavalry — in reality, dragoons — against Indians in the Southwest.

Captain José de Berróteran commanded at Conchos and at Mapima for 35 years. He made a report in 1748 to the viceroy on the cmapaigns he and others had made in the area. The report also contained a series of recommendations on the location of presidios along the Conchos and Del Norte (Rio Grande) rivers.

See locations on the map opposite page 80.

San Sabá, cuya compañia se ha retirado á este fin de la mision del cañon, donde se hallaba, á la citada villa de San Fernando.

17. Como al mismo paso que se hagan los reconocimientos espresados, y el nuevo establecimiento de los cuatro presidios sobre las inmediaciones del rio del Norte, es preciso batir todo el pais que media entre él y la inútil y desguarnecida Frontera, que actualmente forman los tres del Cerro Gordo, Monclova y Santa Rosa, cuidará el comandante de la Nueva Vizcaya de destacar partidas suficientes, mandadas por oficiales de su satisfaccion, para no dejar enemigos á la espalda, y arrojarlos á la otra parte del citado Rio Grande, sin consentir con ningun pretesto que los Apaches Lupanes, queden en el distrito de Coahuila, ni se acojan al abrigo del presidio de San Juan Bautista.

San Juan Bautista.

18. Este presidio que está situado á una legua del mismo rio del Norte, y se halla en la correspondiente altura, debe quedar en el parage que ocupa, completándose su compañia hasta el número señalado á todas las de Frontera, á fin de que sus destacamentos se opongan á las muchas avenidas y pasos vadeables que tiene por su frente y cercanías, y que cruzándose con los de la Monclova y los de San Antonio de Bejar, que han de ser sus colindantes, impidan las invasiones de los enemigos; quedando prevenido, que los diez indios señalados en calidad de exploradores á cada compañia de este presidio, y los demás de la línea desde el de San Buenaventura, se han de elegir de los Julimeños, por su espíritu guerrero y experimentada vizarría.

Bahía del Espíritu Santo.

19. Termina el cordon de presidios de Frontera en el de la Bahía del Espíritu Santo, perteneciente á la provincia de Tejas. Y mando, que por ahora subsista en el parage donde se halla situado, con el mismo destino de su ereccion y el de auxiliarse mutuamente sus destacamentos con los de la villa de San Antonio de Bejar, que sin embargo de estar mas de un grado fuera de la línea, no conviene retirarla por los graves inconvenientes que se seguirán de esta providencia.

San Antonio de Bejar.

20. Mas de un grado de latitud fuera de la línea propuesta está situada la villa de San Antonio de Bejar, en casi igual distancia de los dos presidios referidos de San Juan Bautista y Bahía del Espíritu Santo, y siendo el parage mas espuesto en la actualidad á las invasiones y correrías de varias naciones de indios guerreros del Norte, que hostilizan aquel vecindario sus haciendas y opulentas misiones, con el motivo de perseguir los Apaches Lipanes, que son sus aborrecidos enemigos, y á fin de reforzar segun conviene la espresada poblacion, mando se aumente su compañia hasta el pie que espresa el reglamento, estableciendo allí su residencia el gobernador que antes tenia en el

17. At the same time that the said reconnaissances are underway and the four new presidios are being established in the vicinity of the Rio del Norte, it is necessary to strike in all the country between it and the useless and unprotected frontier now formed by the three presidios of Cerro Gordo, Monclova, and Santa Rosa; the commandant of Nueva Vizcaya will take care to send parties of sufficient strength and commanded by officers he knows are satisfactory in order not to leave enemies at the rear and to drive them to the other side of the said Rio Grande, and he is not to consent under any pretext that the Lipan Apaches be allowed to remain in the district of Coahuila nor congregate in the shelter of the presidio of San Juan Bautista.

San Juan Bautista.

18. This presidio, which is situated one league from the same Rio del Norte and is found at the corresponding latitude, should remain at the place it now occupies; its company is to be filled to the full number prescribed for all the frontier presidios in order that its detachments can defend the many avenues and fording places near the front and sides of the presidio. And, in conjunction with the troops from Monclova and those from San Antonio de Béjar, which will be contiguous with this presidio, they can halt the invasions of the enemies; it is to be kept in mind that the ten Indians assigned as scouts for the company in this presidio, and the others in the line from it to San Buenaventura, are to be selected from the Julimeños because of their warlike spirit and tested bravery.

A tribe which had inhabited northeastern Mexico, and in 1737 was gathered into the mission of San Francisco Vizarrón de los Pausanes, Coahuila.

Bahía del Espíritu Santo.

19. The cordon of presidios of the frontier terminates with that of La Bahía del Espíritu Santo, which is under the jurisdiction of the province of Texas. And I order that for now it continue at the place where it is presently situated, with the same goals as when it was erected: its detachments giving mutual aid to those of the villa of San Antonio de Béjar. Despite the fact that this presidio is more than one degree outside the line, it would not be wise to move it back because of the grave results that would follow.

San Antonio de Béjar.

20. More than one degree of latitude outside the proposed line is situated the town of San Antonio de Béjar, almost equally distant from the two aforesaid presidios of San Juan Bautista and Bahía del Espíritu Santo; it is the place most exposed in actuality to the invasions and raids of various tribes of warlike Indians of the north, who attack the haciendas and opulent missions in that vicinity while pursuing the Lipan Apaches, who are their hated enemies. In order that the settlement be adequately protected, I order that its company be reinforced to the level expressed in the regulations and that the residence of the governor, which previously has been in the

This mission was the precursor of the modern city of San Antonio, Texas.

presidio de los Adaes, de cuya compañia y la de Horcoquizac que han de removerse, debe escoger y completar la de dicha villa.

Destacamento del Arroyo del Cíbolo.

21. De esta nueva compañia y al cargo de un teniente de ella se han de destacar 20 hombres, que deberán situarse de pie fijo sobre las orillas del Arroyo del Cíbolo, para resguardar los ranchos pertenecientes á varios vecinos de San Antonio, y dejar menos descubierto el intermedio de casi 50 leguas que hay desde aquella villa al último presidio ya citado de la Bahía del Espíritu Santo, cuyas partidas podrán mutuamente auxiliarse del referido destacamento, y de comun acuerdo impedir las entradas de los enemigos que puedan recalar por aquel distrito, supuesto que poco ó nada tienen que recelar de los gentiles que habitan hácia las Marismas, por su pusilanimidad y miseria.

22. Prevenida ya la estincion del presidio de San Sabá, para establecer uno de su nombre sobre las orillas del Rio del Norte, y en el supuesto de ser inútiles actualmente los otros dos del Horcoquizac, y los Adaes, ordeno al gobernador de Tejas y demás oficiales de estos dos presidios, que desde luego los desguarnezcan, y abandonen los parages en que se hallan, cuidando de que los pocos vecinos que hay en ellos se retiren á la espresada villa de San Antonio de Bejar, ó sus inmediaciones, donde mando, se les repartan tierras para su establecimiento y subsistencia, y que estingan tambien al propio tiempo las inútiles misiones de Nacodoches, Aes y demás que se han mantenido sin indios algunos á la sombra de los dichos presidios: que se reformen los oficiales y soldados sobrantes de estos, quedando suprimidos sus sueldos y los sínodos de las referidas misiones, en favor de mi real hacienda.

Nueva México.

23. El presidio mas avanzado hácia el Norte y que hace Frontera separada, es el de la Nueva México, cuya remota provincia se halla aislada y sola, pero con bastantes fuerzas en sus muchos pueblos y en la buena calidad de sus vecindarios, por lo que quedando la compañia de Santa Fé sobre el pie señalado en el reglamento, mando que de ellos se destaquen treinta hombres al mando de uno de los tenientes, y se sitúen en el parage nombrado de Robledo, sobre las orillas del Rio Grande del Norte, distante veinte leguas del pueblo del Paso, para que reforzado con treinta vecinos auxiliares, que se reclutarán en este, sirvan á guarnecer el camino que sube por aquella parte, escoltar los cordones de arrieros y pasageros, y oponerse á las avenidas de las naciones bárbaras, que por uno y otro lado recalan hasta el citado rio.

24. A estos vecinos auxiliares se les asistirá con quince pesos mensuales, dinero en mano durante el tiempo de diez años, con la obligacion de concurrir alternativamente á todas las salidas que hiciese la tropa, y de tener á este fin tres caballos y el armamento correspondiente á soldados, pues se les han de pasar revistas como á ellos con

presidio of Los Adaes, be moved there; the companies from Los Adaes and Horcoquisac are to be moved to San Antonio, and from them will be recruited the troops to complete that of the said villa.

Detachment of Arroyo del Cíbolo.

21. From this new company a detachment of 20 men, in the charge of a lieutenant of that company, will be stationed permanently on the banks of the Arroyo del Cíbolo in order to guard the ranches belonging to various inhabitants of San Antonio and to make less vulnerable the intervening area of almost 50 leagues between that villa and the last presidio mentioned above. La Bahía del Espíritu Santo; parties from that presidio and from the aforesaid detachment can render mutual aid to one another, and by their common accord can impede the penetrations of the enemies that filter into that district. It is understood that little or nothing is to be feared from the heathens that inhabit the area toward Las Marismas because of their pusillanimity and wretchedness.

22. Having already decided upon the extinction of the presidio of San Sabá in order to establish one of that name on the banks of the Rio del Norte, and believing the other two of Horcoquisac and Los Adaes to be useless in actuality, I order the governor of Texas and the other officers of those two presidios to remove the troops at once and to abandon the sites where they are located, taking care that the few settlers who live around them retire to the aforesaid villa of San Antonio de Béjar or its vicinity, where I order land to be distributed to them for their settlement and subsistence. And I also order extinguished the useless missions of Nacogdoches, Ais, and the others that are maintained without any Indians in the shadow of the said presidios. And I order that the officers and soldiers attached to these presidios be reassigned, their salaries and the stipends of the aforesaid missions reverted to my royal treasury.

New Mexico.

23. The presidio farthest north, and which forms a separate frontier, is that of New Mexico. That remote province is isolated and alone, but has sufficient strength in its many towns and in the good quality of its inhabitants. Therefore, while the company of Santa Fé will remain on the footing signified by the regulations, I order that thirty men from it be detached under the command of one of the lieutenants and stationed at the place named Robledo, located on the banks of the Rio Grande del Norte 20 leagues distant from the town of El Paso. It will be reinforced with 30 civilian auxiliaries, who will be recruited at that town and will serve to guard the road that passes through that place, escorting the trains of muleteers and travelers and obstructing the avenues of the barbarous nations who on one side or the other filter as far as the said river.

 Santa Fe, New Mexico retains more Spanish colonial atmosphere than other American cities.

24. These civilian auxiliaries will be recompensed with fifteen pesos monthly, cash in hand, for a period of ten years. In return they will be obligated to join, in turn, all sorties made by the troops and to maintain for this purpose three horses and the armament corresponding to soldiers; and like the soldiers they will be required to pass reviews with

regularidad y frecuencia, bien que han de estar exceptuados dichos vecinos del servicio diario del cuartel. Y mando que se les repartan tierras en su inmediacion con la posible igualdad, para que cumpliendo el plazo de los diez años en que deben gozar el prest señalado, se hallen arraigados y en disposicion de sostenerse por sí mismos.

25. Con la idea de facilitar el paso y comunicacion á la citada provincia de la Nueva México, que desde el parage de Robledo, que ha de guarnecerse, hasta su primera débil poblacion de las Nutrias, dista ciento y veinte leguas, prevengo y mando al actual gobernador y sus succesores, que procuren ir restableciendo los arruinados pueblos de Senecu, Socorro, Alamillo y Sevilleta, situados sobre el camino real que sube á Santa Fé, para que en esta forma quede reducido á menos de treinta leguas el intermedio despoblado desde el dicho sitio de Robledo hasta el nombrado de Fr. Cristobal, que por su falta de agua se conoce con el nombre de la Jornada del muerto.

26. A cada uno de los habilitados de los doce presidios que han de trasladarse á formar la línea de los quince espresados, se les librará en las respectivas cajas además del situado, la cantidad de cuatro mil pesos para costear la nueva construccion del recinto que debe ocupar cada uno en el parage que se le señalare; y de dos mil pesos á cada uno de los habilitados de Santa Fé y San Antonio de Bejar, para la construccion de los recintos que han de guarnecer los destacamentos de Robledo y del Arroyo del Cíbolo; pues á fin de facilitar su pronta mutacion, y que la fabrica se haga con arreglo al nuevo plan, se ha de formar primero el cuadro de tápias comunes de adobes, y los dos pequeños baluartes en sus ángulos, y despues levantar en lo interior la capilla, cuerpo de guardia, casa del capitan, oficiales, capellan y habitaciones de los soldados é indios, guareciéndose todos entre tanto en tiendas de campaña y Barracas provisionales, sobre cuyo asunto procederán los capitanes y oficiales subalternos con toda actividad y vigilancia, á que están obligados por sus empleos y honor; y los referidos habilitados llevarán cuenta individual y exacta de lo que efectivamente se comprare para la obra; en inteligencia, de que este trabajo debe hacerlo la guarnicion como faena de campaña, y que cede en su beneficio y defensa, sin recargar á los indios exploradores con mas fatiga que á los soldados, por debérseles tratar con igualdad, y darse á todos una moderada gratificacion por este extraordinario trabajo, que regulará y firmará el capitan, con intervencion y acuerdo de sus oficiales subalternos.

Nuevo Reino de Leon.

27. Con atencion á que la ciudad de Monterey, capital del Nuevo Reino de Leon, no se halla ya espuesta á invasiones de enemigos, y que su vecindario, con los de las poblaciones dependientes, son muy bastantes á defenderse por sí mismos en cualquiera caso, cumpliendo con las obligaciones que contrajeron al tiempo de su establecimiento, mando á mi virey reforme el presidio existente en la espresada capital de Monterey, compuesto de un capitan, teniente, alferez, sargento

regularity and frequency, although the said civilians are to be excepted from daily garrison duties. And I order that land in the vicinity be divided among them with all possible impartiality so that at the end of their ten-year terms, during which they receive the aforesaid pay, they will be firmly established and able to sustain themselves.

25. With the idea of facilitating travel and communication to the said province of New Mexico, I decree and order the present governor and his successors to work to re-establish the ruined towns of Senecu, Socorro, Alamillo, and Sevilleta, which are situated along the *camino real* that runs to Santa Fé and which are between the post of Robledo, soon to be garrisoned, and the weak settlement of Las Nutrias, distant one hundred and twenty leagues; in this way the intervening unpopulated area between the said place of Robledo to that named Fray Cristobal will be reduced to less than thirty leagues, a stretch that for lack of water has come to be known by the name of the Journey of Death.

26. To each one of the paymasters of the twelve presidios that are to be moved to form the line of fifteen will be delivered at the respective treasuries, above the normal allowance, the quantity of four thousand pesos to pay for the construction of the new buildings which each one should have at its designated site; and two thousand pesos will be delivered to the paymasters at Santa Fé and San Antonio de Béjar for the construction of the buildings to be garrisoned by the detachments at Robledo and Arroyo del Cíbolo. In order to facilitate this change promptly and that the buildings be done in accordance with the new plan, the exterior walls are to be built first of adobes, with two small bastions in the angles; afterward on the interior will be built the chapel, the guardhouse, residences for the captain, officers, and chaplain, and quarters for the soldiers and Indians, sheltering everyone during the construction in campaign tents and temporary barracks. In this matter the captain and subaltern officers will apply themselves with all possible diligence and watchfulness, as they are obligated to do by their rank and their honor; and the aforesaid paymasters will keep a detailed and exact account of all they actually buy for the work. It is understood that this work should be done by the troops as a campaign task and that it will accrue to their benefit and protection; the Indian scouts are not to be burdened with more work than that of the soldiers, for both should be treated equally. All should be given a moderate gratuity for this special work, as regulated and vouched for by the captain, with the advice and accord of his subaltern officers.

Nuevo Reino de Leon.

27. As for the city of Monterrey, capital of Nuevo Reino de Leon, it is not now exposed to the invasions of enemies, and its inhabitants and those of its dependent settlements are sufficiently numerous to defend themselves in any case whatsoever, thus complying with the obligations that they contracted at the time of their settlement. I order my viceroy to reorganize the presidio that is in the said capital of Monterrey, which as of the last day of this year is composed of a captain, lieutenant, ensign, sergeant,

y veinte y tres soldados, en el dia último de este año; y que desde el primero del idmediato, establezca en las cuatro misiones de su distrito dos salvaguardias en cada una, con el sueldo de doscientos pesos, que siendo ocho, importan mil y seiscientos pesos anuales, que han de cobrar en la caja real de San Luis de Potosí.

Nayarit y su comandante.

28. Esta pequeña provincia, compuesta de asperísimas montañas en que no pueden andar caballos, y habitada por unos naturales débiles, aunque propensos á su antigua idolatría, no necesita de la compañia de presidio que inutilmente se ha mantenido en ella á cargo de un capitan que tambien ejerce la jurisdiccion y funciones de gobernador; y para que los ministros de las siete misiones existentes en aquel distrito tengan un hombre de resguardo que los acompañe, ordeno que reformada desde luego la espresada compañia vacante hoy por muerte del capitan, se establezcan siete salvaguardias en dichas misiones, con el sueldo de doscientos pesos cada una, que ascenderán á mil y cuatrocientos pesos anuales, y se les han de satistacer en la caja real de Guadalajara; pero á fin de mantener en respeto dicha provincia, y que haya sugeto capáz de proveer á lo que ocurra en el reducido gobierno de ella, ordeno y mando á mi virey destine á un oficial subalterno de los voluntarios de Cataluña, ó de los fusileros de Montaña, con un sargento y catorce hombres de su respectiva tropa, que se establecerán en la cabecera nombrada la Mesa de el Tonati, abonándose al referido oficial por la misma caja quinientos pesos de gratificacion al año sobre su sueldo; y si este destacamento que se relevará anualmente, necesitare hacer algunas salidas á marchas apresuradas, le proveerá de mulas del pais, cuyo costo justificada su legitimidad, se abonará tambien por mi real hacienda.

Californias.

29. Arreglados ya los presidios del continente y sus situados anuales (pues los dos interiores de Sonora que solo deben subsistir interín se radican en pueblos los indios rendidos, quedan sujetos en todo á este reglamento), declaro que los de Californias han de continuar por ahora sobre el pié que se hallan, conforme á las providencias dadas por mi virey, despues de haberse estendido la conquista y reduccion hasta el puerto de Monterey; y supuesto de tener provisionalmente señalada la cantidad anual de treinta y tres mil pesos para las atenciones y resguardo de aquella península, ordeno y mando que este situado se continúe, pagando al fin de cada año en la real caja de Guadalajara, como se ha practicado últimamente; y que mi virey sostenga y auxilie por todos los medios posibles los antiguos y nuevos establecimientos de dicha provincia, y me informe de todo lo que regulare conducente y útil para su fomento, pueble y estension de las nuevas reducciones de indios gentiles.

Y siendo mi real voluntad que el contesto de estas determinacio-

and twenty-three soldiers. From the first day of next year two sentries will be posted in the four missions in this district, with a salary of two hundred pesos each; as they are eight in number, their wages will total sixteen hundred pesos annually, a sum to be drawn from the royal treasury at San Luis de Potosí.

Nayarit and its commandant.

28. This small province, made up of steep mountains over which horses cannot travel and inhabited by weak natives who are disposed to their ancient idolatry, does not need the presidial company which uselessly has been maintained there under the command of a captain, who also exercised the jurisdiction and functions of governor; in order that the ministers of the seven extant missions in that district have a guard to accompany each of them, I order that the said company, now vacant because of the death of the captain, be reorganized at once, assigning to the said missions seven sentries with a salary of two hundred pesos each. This will amount to fourteen hundred pesos annually, which will be drawn from the royal treasury at Guadalajara. To maintain peace in the said province and to have someone there capable of coping with whatever may occur in the thus reduced territory, I order and command my viceroy to appoint one subaltern official from the Catalonian Volunteers or the Montaña Fusileers, along with a sergeant and fourteen men of the respective troop, to establish himself in the principal settlement in the district, Mesa de el Tonati; the said officer annually is to receive from the same treasury five hundred pesos above his salary as a gratuity, and this detachment will be relieved annually by another. If any sallies of forced marches are necessary, the needed mules will be procured in the area, and the cost, when justified as legitimate, will likewise be paid by my royal treasury.

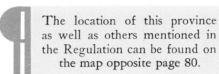

The location of this province as well as others mentioned in the Regulation can be found on the map opposite page 80.

The Californias.

29. Provision having thus been made for the presidios of the mainland, as well as for their annual appropriation (the two interior presidios of Sonora will be maintained only so long as the submissive Indians are being gathered into towns; in the meantime they are subject to all that is in this regulation), and I declare that the presidios of the Californias are to continue on the same footing that they now are, conforming to the decrees given by my viceroy, until the conquest and settlement of the Indians has been completed as far as the port of Monterey; and understanding that the quantity of thirty-three thousand pesos has been provisionally appropriated annually for the care and security of that peninsula, I order and command that this sum continue to be paid at the end of each year at the royal treasury of Guadalajara, as has been the practice in the past, and that my viceroy support and aid by every possible means the old and new settlements in the said province. He is to inform me of all measures he takes conducive and useful to the development, colonization, and extension of new settlements for *gentile* Indians.

Since it is my royal will that the text of these

nes y reglas establecidas se observe, guarde y ejecute, mando á vos mi
virey, gobernador y capitan general del reino y provincias de la Nueva España, sus gobernadores, comandantes, capitanes y subalternos, y
demás personas á quienes pueda tocar y pertenecer, no vayan ni per-
mitan ir, ni contravenir á ellas en manera alguna, y hagais se guar-
den, cumplan y ejecuten sin escusa ni interpretacion; para lo cual he
resuelto establecer el presente reglamento é instruccion, firmado de mi
real mano, sellado con el sello secreto, y refrendado de mi Secretario
de estado y del despacho universal de Indias y Marina. Dado en San
Ildefonso á diez de Septiembre de mil setecientos sesenta y dos—YO
EL REY—D. Julian de Arriaga.

    Es copia de su original.

instructions and rules be observed, enforced, and executed, I order you —my viceroy, governor, and captain-general of the kingdom and province of New Spain; governors, commandants, captains, and subaltern officers; and other persons to whom these regulations may apply and appertain—not to disobey them or to permit them to be disobeyed in any way whatsoever and to see that they are kept, complied with, and executed without excuse or personal interpretation. To this end I have resolved to issue the present regulation and instruction under my royal hand, sealed with my privy seal, and countersigned by my Secretary of State, General Affairs of the Indies, and Navy.

Given in San Ildefonso on September 10, 1772.

I, THE KING

Don Julián de Arriaga

(This is a copy of the original)

Although Mexico had been completely severed from Spain for a dozen years when this edition of the Regulation was printed in 1834, officials of the new republic evidently ordered the king's 1772 version reprinted without changes that should have been made when Mexico became self-governing. A tradition of the Spanish crown thus survived independence.

INDIAN TRIBES AND RAIDING TRAILS ON THE NORTHERN FRONTIER OF NEW SPAIN

PART THREE

Weapons and Equipment
of the Presidial Soldier

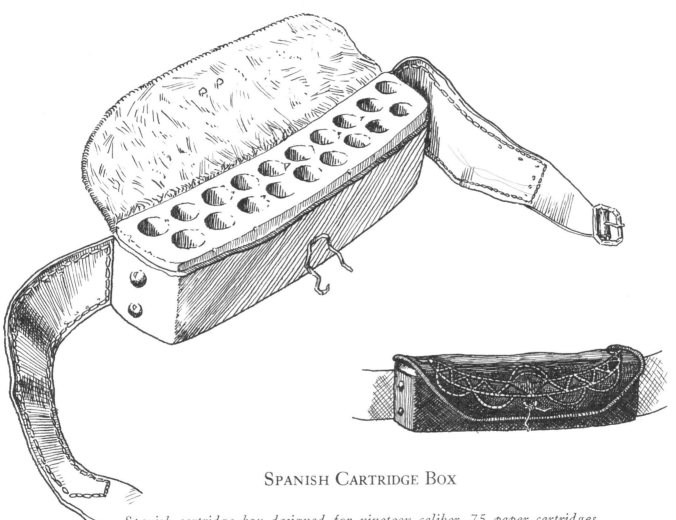

SPANISH CARTRIDGE BOX

Spanish cartridge box designed for nineteen caliber .75 paper cartridges. Worn to the front and buckled to the back, this embroidered specimen is typical of those carried by frontier presidio soldiers during the latter part of the 18th century. Many cartridge boxes issued to frontier soldiers had the arms of Spain embossed on the front flap. One such specimen is in the collection of the Los Angeles County Museum. Pouch in the collection of the MUSEUM OF NEW MEXICO, *Santa Fe. Sketch by* JERRY MARTIN.

PLATE ONE

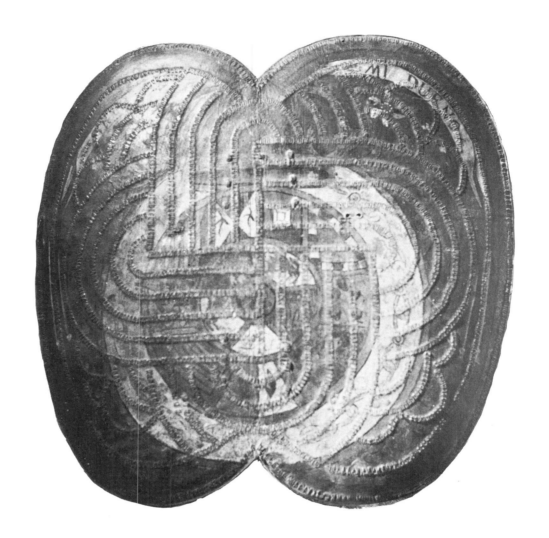

OFFICER'S SHIELD

The 18th century Spanish adarga *or shield was made of three thicknesses of bullhide stitched together and was designed to deflect lance thrusts or arrows. Evolved from a Moorish design of the 13th century, the* adarga *carried by the presidio soldier was generally about 20 inches high and 24 inches across. Officers' shields were often painted with the royal arms of Spain or a family crest. Those of the enlisted men were plain and cost the soldier 30 pesos. The* adarga *was worn on the left arm and carried on the back when not in use. The shield illustrated is a late 18th century officers' model from Durango, Mexico. Photograph by* DR. ARTHUR WOODWARD.

PLATE TWO

Spanish Short Sword

Espada ancha *or wide sword of the type that was carried by the* soldados de cuera. *This crudely fashioned specimen, made with an 18-inch cut-off saber blade, was found in Canyon del Muerto in northeastern Arizona, and dates from about 1800. Many of the short swords were made in the northern provinces and were preferred by its soldiers to the larger cavalry saber. The* espada ancha *was carried in a leather scabbard, attached to the saddle, hilt forward, on the left side, or sometimes on a sling hung over the soldier's right shoulder. Sword from the collection of* LESTER WARD RUFFNER, *Prescott, Arizona. Photograph by* BRUCE D. LINDSAY.

PLATE THREE

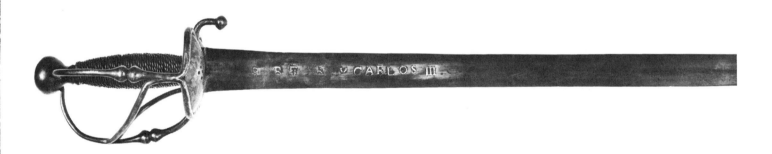

Spanish Cavalry Saber

The Regulations of 1772 specified that a saber of this type be carried by the presidial soldiers. The short wide sword was more popular, but this style also saw use in New Spain. The 36½-inch double-edged straight blade bears the inscription "for King Carlos III" on one side, and on the other, "cavalry, 1774." The hilt is made of iron and the grip is wire wrapped. Sometimes these swords were cut off on the frontier to make the espada ancha. *In the* BRINCKERHOFF COLLECTION *at the* ARIZONA PIONEERS' HISTORICAL SOCIETY, *Tucson.*

PLATE FOUR

[71]

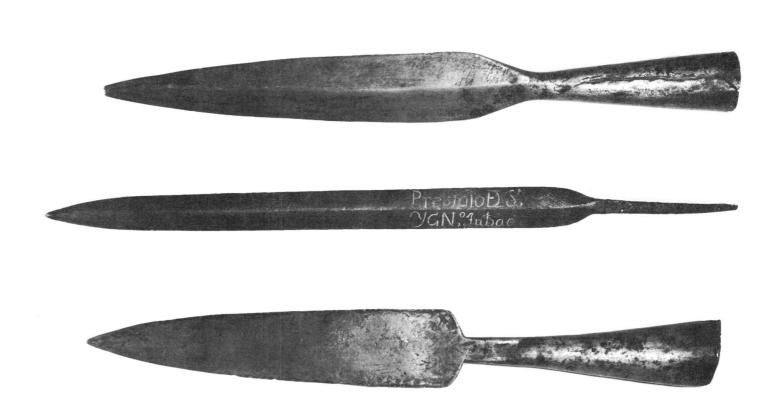

LANCE BLADES

The lance was often the principal weapon of the frontier Spanish soldier. These three blades, of varying lengths, illustrate some of the patterns used in the northern provinces. The center blade, 12 inches long, is stamped with the name of the Presidio of Tubac, now incorporatd into a State Park in southern Arizona. Mounted on the end of eight-foot lances these blades were vicious weapons when used by competent soldiers. Top and bottom blades from the JAMES E. SERVEN COLLECTION, *Tucson. The center blade is from the* TUBAC STATE PARK MUSEUM, *Tubac, Arizona. Photograph by* BRUCE D. LINDSAY.

PLATE FIVE

[72]

Spanish Escopeta

The escopeta, *a light, smoothbore, muzzle-loading musket or carbine was a popular weapon of the 18th century* soldado de cuera. *Made with a Spanish or* miguelet *lock and a Catalan stock, this sturdy and dependable weapon saw use for nearly 200 years on the northern frontier. There were many variations in barrel length, and stock design, but the* miguelet *lock was commonly used. In 1786,* escopetas *purchased for frontier use cost the Crown 6 pesos, 5 reales, 9 grains. The model illustrated was made by Antonio Guisasola of Eibar, Spain, about 1800. It is caliber .75 with a Catalan stock and a 33½-inch barrel. The quality of the piece indicates that it was carried by a gentleman or officer. This* escopeta *is in the* WILLIAM RENWICK COLLECTION, *Tucson. Photograph by* BRUCE D. LINDSAY.

PLATE SIX

English Military Carbine

English Tower flintlock carbine of about 1812. Military carbines and muskets of Spanish, French and English manufacture were in use on the northern frontier during the late Spanish period and were purchased by the Mexicans particularly from the British and used by their cavalry into the 1850's. Now .80 caliber with a short, 22-inch barrel, this smoothbore weapon was usually called an escopeta. *In the collection of the* ARIZONA PIONEERS' HISTORICAL SOCIETY, *Tucson. Photo by* BRUCE D. LINDSAY.

PLATE SEVEN

[73]

INDIAN TRADE MUSKET

Trade musket of the pattern that was popular with Spain's Indian enemies. This specimen, an American copy of the English North West Company trade gun, was made by H. Leman of Lancaster, Pennsylvania, and has false English proof marks. It is light weight and made in caliber .56 with a 36-inch barrel. The brass tacks were added by a former Indian owner. From the JAMES E. SERVEN COLLECTION, *Tucson. Photo by the owner.*

PLATE EIGHT

MIGUELET LOCK

Miguelet *lock on a typical* escopeta, *found in New Mexico. The stock is a locally-made replacement of Catalan design. This specimen is .60 caliber smoothbore, and has a 33½-inch barrel. It dates from about 1790. In the collection of the* MUSEUM OF NEW MEXICO, *Santa Fe. Photograph provided by the Museum.*

PLATE NINE

[74]

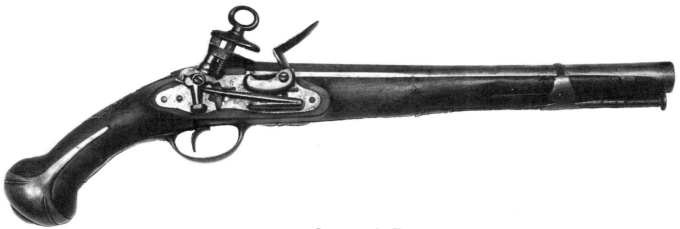

SOLDIER'S PISTOL

Spanish mounted soldier's miguelet *lock pistol of about 1780. By regulation, each presidial soldier carried two of these pistols. This one has a 12½-inch barrel, is .70 caliber, and has brass fittings, including a plaque bearing the arms of Spain mounted on the back of the grip. From the* WILLIAM REN-WICK COLLECTION, *Tucson. Photograph by* BRUCE D. LINDSAY.

PLATE TEN

OFFICER'S PISTOL

Well-made engraved pistols such as this one were carried by some of the presidio officers. Made by Matias Baeza of Madrid in 1703, this Madrid lock *horseman's pistol is caliber .62, smoothbore, with a 12½-inch barrel and engraved silver trim. It was found in Durango, Mexico. Owned by* MARY GALLEGOS DE HILLARY, *Tucson.*

PLATE ELEVEN

Spanish Cannon

Spanish light swivel cannon of the type used on the walls of presidios in the 18th century. This bronze 4-pounder is mounted on a crude 2-foot high naval type carriage and was found at a Spanish fort on Mindanao Island in the Philippines. In 1768, Fronteras, Terrenate, and Tubac in Sonora each had four 4-pounders, cast in Mexico, which were reported to be virtually useless. The cannon illustrated is owned by the Arizona State Museum, University of Arizona, *Tucson. Photograph by* Bruce D. Lindsay.

Plate Twelve

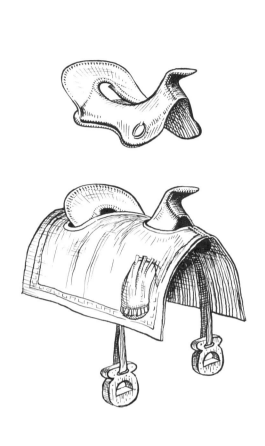

PLATE THIRTEEN   PLATE FOURTEEN

VAQUERO SADDLE AND TRAPPINGS

The saddle commonly used by the soldiers on the frontier had a hardwood tree, with a rawhide cover, sewn and shrunk to the tree. Down over the bow and cantle was placed a large, soft leather covering known as a coraza, *and overall, a smaller leather pad or mo-chila, which sometimes held front-mounted saddle bags, or* coginillos. *The illustration shows the saddle bags mounted on a single saddle cover. Also in use was an* anguera *or smaller* anguerita, *decorated armor rump covering for the horse made of seven panels of leather attached to the back of the saddle. To protect the soldier's legs from the harsh brush of the frontier country,* armas, *or side skirts of leather hung from the saddle over the rider's legs to below the stirrups, tied at the bow and cantle. When not in use, the* armas *were tied only to the front of the saddle and gave some protection to the horse's front legs and shoulders. Stirrups normally were made locally of wood, and often came equipped with leather* tapaderas, *or covers, over the front. Saddle in the collection of the* ARIZONA PIONEERS' HISTORICAL SOCIETY, *Tucson.*

[77]

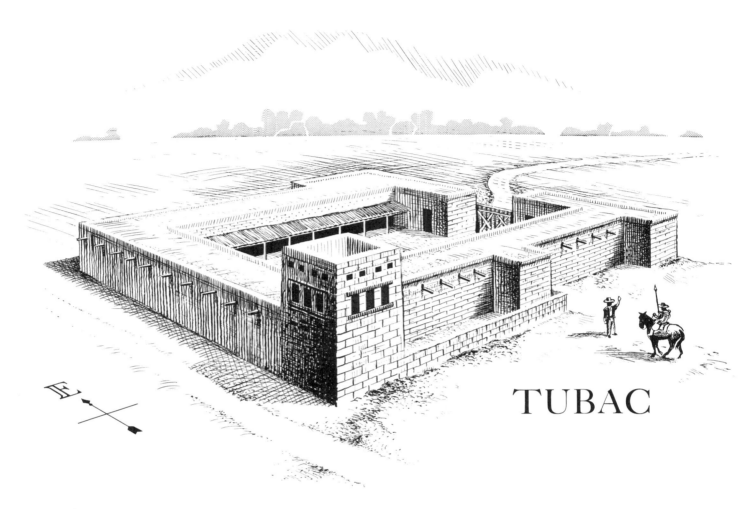

TUBAC

The Presidio of Tubac, Spanish province of Sonora, about 1770. Most presidios were built of sun-dried adobe brick, and designed to surround one or more courtyards. Doors and windows opened onto the courtyard while the outside walls were made without openings for protection. Square or round towers were built at the corners and served as firing platforms for muskets and even small cannon. The soldiers and their families lived inside the fort, which also was a refuge for the settlers and their animals when Indians attacked. Often complete with a church and shops, these Spanish frontier forts were actually walled towns. Artist's conception by DON BUFKIN, *Tucson.*

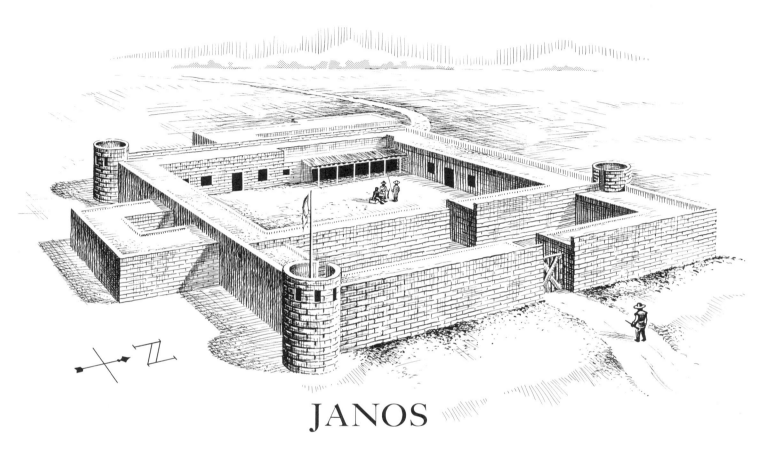

JANOS

*The Presidio of Janos, Spanish province of Nueva Vizcaya, about 1780.
The walls and left tower in the foreground were not part of the original
structure. When first built, the presidio had the usual four walls with
two round towers at opposite corners. The third tower was added to defend
the new front gate created by expanded walls and courtyard area. Artist's
conception by* Don Bufkin, *Tucson.*

PART FOUR

The Spanish Military System in the Interior Provinces: *An Appraisal*

In studying the problem of defending the Interior Provinces from the attacks of savage Indians, high Spanish officials placed much stress on the precise locations of the presidios. The Marqués de Rubí and José de Gálvez both declared that the frontier could be controlled more effectively by relocating the presidios at 40-league intervals in a cordon that would stretch from the Gulf of California to the Gulf of Mexico. However, these officials overlooked the basic fact that the precise locations of the presidios would prove of less importance than the competence of the soldiers garrisoning them. It was the fighting capacity of each private, corporal, sergeant, and officer that was to mean the difference between victory and defeat in engagements with hostile Indians, not the exact site of a particular fort. And defeat came more often than victory in the Interior Provinces.

The presidial system was only one of the three separate but related colonial institutions employed by Imperial Spain on the northern frontier. The other two were the mission and the civil settlement. On paper these institutions seemed excellent. Missionaries venturing into the wilderness would spread the gospel of Christianity among the heathen savages. Those converted would be gathered into missions—self-contained religious units where the natives would till fields, herd cattle, and learn arts and crafts. The Indians thus would become civilized—and Hispanicized—by their Franciscan or Jesuit tutors. The missionaries would be protected by soldiers, who would be housed in presidios near the missions. These troops would provide the physical strength needed to overawe the natives, but force would be used only when necessary to coerce the heathens into a receptive attitude toward the teachings of the missionaries. And the families of the soldiers would be sent to the frontier with them, merchants would come to sell them goods, while farmers and ranchers would be given land in the vicinity. Thus civil settlements, recognized by law, would grow near the presidios and missions. Through this process a three-pronged attack would be made on the wilderness to bring it under Spanish domination.

For the most part, however, the mission system was a failure. In Arizona the Western Apache bands did not take to mission life, nor did their eastern kinsmen in New Mexico and Texas or the lordly Comanches in Texas submit to the gentle persuasions of the padres.

The only successes enjoyed by the missionaries were among sedentary tribes such as the Pimas and Ópatas of Sonora, the Papagos of Arizona, the Pueblo Indians of New Mexico, and the Hasinai Confederacy of East Texas. Yet even these normally peaceful tribes occasionally rebelled, martyred their missionaries, burned the religious establishments, and fled to wilderness hideouts. In 1751, for example, the Pimas staged a bloody uprising, as had New Mexican natives in 1680 and the Tejas Indians in 1693.

Even when they did not rise in revolt, the mission Indians used the slightest pretext to flee from the rigid confines of the padres' care. A native leader, growing tired of the mission or becoming jealous of the missionaries' influence among his people, would persuade the others that their old way of life was better, that the old gods were more powerful, or that the Spaniards were abusing them. Then the converts would slip away from their mission station to return to their former haunts. Soldiers in nearby presidios often harmed the missionary effort more than they helped it; they killed the cattle sent to feed the natives, they lived riotous lives, and they mistreated the natives—all of which caused aposticizing. Likewise, the wild Indians still in the vicinity of the missions were a powerful deterrent to success. The Comanches and the Apaches found the religious establishments easy prey for their depredations and a convenient and rich source of booty. The mere rumor that raiding parties from either of these nations were coming was usually enough to cause wholesale desertions among the converts.

Another weakness in the mission system was the low birth rate among the neophytes. Sociologists have noted that when the culture of a native people is suddenly altered drastically, they have fewer children. Such was the case in the Spanish missions in northern New Spain. For example, the census for Texas in 1783 shows that 861 Spanish men and women had 716 children, whereas 531 adult mission Indians had only 146 children.[1] Thus the Indians gathered under missionary tutelage were not self-perpetuating. Desertions and the low ratio of children made constant recruiting a necessity, while Comanche and Apache hostility rendered such recruiting not only difficult but also hazardous. Because of the poor results during the initial phase of missionary effort, the Spanish government was unwilling during the last years of the colonial era to finance the continued struggle for converts; it turned instead to military coercion to secure peace.

Nor did the civil settlements work as planned. At the end of the Spanish colonial era, there were only a few scattered towns on the northern frontier. In Texas were San Antonio, La Bahía, and Nacogdoches. Arizona had only Tucson and Tubac. New Mexico boasted more villages than the other two areas combined; but even in that province

---

[1]Domingo Cabello, "*Estado que manifiesta el Numero de Vasallos, y Habitantes que tiene el en esta probincia . . . ,*" December 31, 1783, San Antonio, Béxar Archives (University of Texas Archives, Austin).

there was little security for life or property because of Indian incursions, and more settlers were petitioning for permission to leave than there were recruits coming in. California had few civil settlements because of the difficulties of reaching it; the Yuma Indians had risen in rebellion in 1781 and had cut off overland communication with the province by way of the Anza-Garcés route.

In all four areas the civil settlements existed for the most part in the shadows of the presidios where the civilians could quickly gather when raids occurred. These civilians usually were timorous, impoverished peasants. They could have land almost for the asking, but ownership carried with it an obligation to keep arms and horses ready to assist the military when expeditions were necessary. Spanish authorities envisioned the male civilian population as a standing militia, a source of additional military strength in times of danger. But such was not the case. Settlers proved more a source of weakness than of strength; most of them would not join in forays against the enemy, and yet they had to be protected.

By 1772 the task of conquering and civilizing the area that came to be the American Southwest had fallen almost entirely on the regular soldiers of the presidial establishments. And here again the system largely failed. Spanish records of the late 18th century are filled with accounts of military setbacks all along the presidial line. On February 24, 1773, for example, Apaches struck at Tubac, killed one soldier, and stole more than 100 horses. Early in 1774 they raided Tubac again, captured 100 head of cattle, and killed a sergeant. In May of that same year Gila Apaches besieged Fronteras in such numbers and with such ferocity that the troops there retreated within the walls of their fort, leaving the savages free to drive off the entire presidial herd of 300 horses—and the commandant reported that, as usual, pursuit of the raiders proved fruitless. Late in 1774 at Fronteras 14 soldiers were killed in a skirmish with Apaches.[2]

Between 1772 and 1776 Commandant-Inspector Hugo O'Conor took vigorous steps against the natives committing the raids. In the fall of 1775 he conducted an offensive all along the frontier between Sonora and Texas. In a campaign that involved 1,228 soldiers, he achieved some positive results, just as he did the following year in a similar offensive.[3]

[2]Alfred B. Thomas, *Forgotten Frontiers: A Study of the Spanish Indian Policy of Don Juan Bautista de Anza, Governor of New Mexico, 1777-1787* (Norman: University of Oklahoma Press, 1932), 9.

"The early discoverers won a great part of the Kingdom in little time because the zeal, fervor, and valor of the troops were of a different sort. In the beginning one Spaniard was match enough for twenty or thirty Indians: at present one Indian is enough for ten and even twenty Spanish soldiers." Father Josef Soler to Father Guardian Romauldo Cartagena, San Diego del Pitic, August 12, 1773. A.D.S. in Fra Marcellino Da Civezza Collection, University of Arizona Library, Tucson.

[3]*Ibid.*, 10-13. During the campaign of 1775, as so often happened when the Spaniards were in the field, the Apaches made frequent raids on the towns left virtually undefended by the troops in the field. Alfred B. Thomas, *Teodoro de Croix and the Northern Frontier of New Spain, 1776-1783* (Norman: University of Oklahoma Press, 1941), 14.

Yet despite such victories, the reports show that between 1771 and 1776 in Nueva Vizcaya alone there were 1,674 persons murdered, 154 captured, 116 haciendas abandoned and 68,256 head of livestock stolen.[4]

To remedy this deplorable situation, the Interior Provinces in 1776 were designated a separate political and military unit under the command of Brigadier Teodoro de Croix as commandant-general. A native of France who had entered the Spanish army at the age of 17, Croix was a veteran of many engagements in Europe. He had come to New Spain in 1766 with his uncle, the Marqués de Croix, the newly appointed viceroy. For four years he served in the Kingdom of New Spain, then in 1770 returned to Spain where he remained until his appointment as commandant-general of the Interior Provinces was conferred. Croix's loyalty to the Spanish crown had been proven, his ability was a matter of record, and his courage was unquestioned. He was an excellent choice for the difficult work at hand.

As commandant-general it was Croix's formidable task to halt the shrinkage of the area under Spanish control on the northern frontier. He was given no additional funds or regiments for this undertaking. Instead, he had to cope with the problems by shifting his available troops to those locations where they were most needed. By various devices Croix tried to increase the number of regulars at critical points. Catalonian infantry volunteers were brought to Nueva Vizcaya, as were dragoons from the regular army, but regular cavalry units in Mexico City and Guadalajara, while desperately needed in the north, were not released for his use.[5] Yet by 1783 Croix could report that total military strength in the Interior Provinces was at the highest point in history. A total of 4,686 men—regulars, militia, and Indian allies—were now stationed between Sonora and Texas, ready for service in the field.[6]

Still, the commandant-general noted, Apaches and Comanches frequently struck at the military horse herds pastured outside the presidios, and the detachments guarding these animals usually offered little resistence to the fast-moving, well-armed raiders. Thus the Indians could drive off the herds almost at will. Presidial captains consequently could not retaliate against the marauding savages when their troops were left afoot. Since it took from three to six months to get replacements from the interior of Mexico, the commandant-general suggested that the presidial herds be stabled inside the forts; but so little feed was available within the enclosures that the old system prevailed after his recommendation—with the same result.[7]

---

[4]Thomas, *Teodoro de Croix*, 31.

[5]*Ibid.*, 32, 64.

[6]*Ibid.*, 67. The most dependable Indian allies of the Spaniards in the Interior Provinces were the Ópatas of Sonora, one of the few tribes on the frontier that took readily to mission life.

[7]Alfred B. Thomas, *The Plains Indians and New Mexico, 1751-1778* (Albuquerque: University of New Mexico Press, 1940), 42, 204. For a specific example, see Cabello to Commandant-general Philipe de Neve, No. 852, December 20, 1784, San Antonio, Béxar Archives.

Croix also urged a decrease in the number of horses each soldier took on campaigns. Normally each trooper took six horses and two or three mules with him for riding and carrying supplies. With such a large remuda stirring up dust, surprise attacks against Indian camps were almost impossible. Forewarned, the Indians frequently stampeded the animals. Presidial captains continued to insist to the commandant-general that desert campaigns required frequent changes of mounts, but Croix replied that a few well-fed horses would prove far more useful than a large number of half-starved animals. Yet because horse traders enjoyed a brisk business supplying the presidios with replacements, no serious reduction in the size of the herds ever was made.[8]

Croix, his subordinates, and his successors found that their every effort at serious reform in the Interior Provinces was hampered by inadequate financial support from Mexico City and Madrid. There simply was not enough gold in the royal treasury for all the demands made upon it—especially for such an elaborate program of defense as the frontier situation demanded. During most of the 18th and in the first years of the 19th centuries, Spain was involved in a series of costly conflicts and intrigues in Europe. Between 1701 and 1713 raged the War of the Spanish Succession, in which the grandson of Louis XIV of France, Philip of Anjou, finally gained the Spanish throne. Philip and his successors dutifully went to war on the side of France in the War of the Austrian Succession (1744-1748) and again in the Seven Years' War (1756-1763). Following the ruinous defeat of France in the latter struggle, Spain obtained title to the province of Louisiana as compensation for her losses elsewhere; and the acquisition of this vast domain west of the Mississippi River now necessitated the sweeping changes in policy recommended by Visitor-General José de Gálvez and the Marqués de Rubí.

Then came the American Revolution, and when France joined cause with the Americans the Spanish Bourbon ruler followed where his French cousin led. Fifteen years later Spain sided with England in resisting the radical doctrines of liberty and equality being exported from revolutionary France, but in 1796 the Spaniards decided to ally with the Republic of France in a war against England. The tenuous Franco-Spanish accord lasted until 1808 when Napoleon ordered his troops into the Iberian peninsula, whereupon Spain once more joined England and fought the French until Napoleon's final downfall. Thus the larger exigencies of international affairs diverted the attention of the Spanish rulers from the New World to the Old, and neither sufficient men nor money could be made available for such distant responsibilities as frontier defense against raiding Comanches and Apaches and the establishment of new settlements in the remote reaches of Sonora, New Mexico, and Texas. The very best that Spain could do for these far areas was to retrench and reorganize—mostly on paper—and to send a few good officers to positions of high command.

---

[8]Thomas, *Teodoro de Croix*, 57.

In their attempts to cure the ills of the Interior Provinces, these officers were hindered not only by the inadequate royal support but also by problems of supply. Since England dominated the seas throughout the 18th century, trade goods and military supplies could not be brought easily to northern New Spain. In addition, the serpentine workings of the Spanish mercantile economy, with its multiplicity of taxes and its bureaucratic restrictions, meant that goods which did arrive were so costly that they could not compete with French, American, and English goods introduced by smugglers.. A number of government officials, including a few governors, were convicted of smuggling goods into the Interior Provinces, but convictions of those caught did not seem to deter others from illicitly supplying the demand. When Spain finally turned to a policy of conciliating the Indians by an annual distribution of presents, officers on the frontier often found that they had to buy such goods from foreigners—in effect breaking the laws of their country in order to procure the gifts guaranteed by law for the Indian wards.

Officials in the Interior Provinces also were confronted, during the last years of Spanish control, with the threat of illegal entrance by a multitude of adventurers from the United States — adventurers whose ambition it was to take territory that belonged to Spain. The first of these was the enigmatic Philip Nolan — like his celebrated fictional namesake a "man without a country"—who was killed near the present site of Waco, Texas, in 1801. Then came the Gutiérrez-Magee expedition of 1812-1813, followed by Luis Aury, Jean Lafitte, Dr. James Long, and others. Therefore the Spaniards not only had to overcome the natives and subdue their own revolutionaries, such as the priests Miguel Hidalgo and José María Morelos, but also had to contend with foreign opportunists or filibusters.

These factors alone do not explain the numerous reverses suffered by Spanish soldiers on the frontier, however. Nor can their unimpressive performance be explained by racial factors. Some writers have attributed the poor showing of Spanish troops to the alleged laziness or cowardice of the mixed-bloods, or *mestizos,* who constituted the largest racial group among the enlisted men in the frontier army. The distinguished Texas historian, Walter Prescott Webb, contends in his classic work, *The Great Plains,* that racial factors explain the incompetence of the Spaniards as fighting men. Writers such as Webb have found support for this argument in the statements of high-born European officers who commanded in the Interior Provinces. These officers frequently made derogatory judgments of the provincials under their command, and modern scholars have tended to accept this 18th-century prejudice without question. Yet these same *mestizos* attained the military skill necessary to overthrow Spanish rule and win independence from their European masters.

Actually the lower-class citizen of New Spain who enlisted in the army for service in the Interior Provinces came to his post with great potential. In the majority of cases he had been born on that frontier and thus was accustomed to the harsh desert climate and was an expert horseman.[9] He had been so subjected to governmental discipline all his life that he could regard soldiering as the best life available to him. A soldier in the Spanish army had retirement benefits, a pension for his widow in case of his death, and the right to skilled medical attention. There also was the bright hope of promotion, for most junior officers in the Interior Provinces had been raised from the ranks. Additionally, the soldier could easily obtain land near the presidio for himself and his family during his 10-year enlistment. The laws also encouraged him to remain permanently on these acres following his discharge.[10] Finally, the soldier had high social standing. His was a vital and necessary function in a society that in actuality was a military hierarchy—his captain not only performed military duties, but also was the chief executive, the highest judge, and the *jefe político* in the area. Soldiering was an honorable profession.

If racial factors do not explain the weakness of the Spanish frontier army, other logical answers must be sought. Nicolás de Lafora, the engineer who accompanied Rubí, and Commandant-General Croix felt that the explanation for the ineffectiveness of the troops was the presidial captains. Lafora in 1768 resoundingly condemned the captains along the frontier, accusing them of indolence, ignorance, and inexperience. Ten years later Croix said of these officers: "Very few give any hope of improving their behavior and conduct. They openly embrace all the abominable excesses, . . . do not observe orders, [and] hide the truth . . . I have no others to whom to turn."[11] Where possible Croix appointed new presidial commanders, but always he was plagued by a shortage of competent officers. Therefore he circulated a handbook of the penal laws, with orders that these be read to the soldiers every six months. He also sent a list of instructions to all officers for the training of troops in field maneuvers and in the handling of weapons.

In this last measure Croix hit close to the cause of the ineffectiveness and came near finding a cure for it. Poor training and improper weapons in large part accounted for the many defeats suffered by the Spaniards in the Interior Provinces. In general, recruits were subjected to no fixed training program, were given poor mounts and inadequate equipment, and often were commanded by indolent and corrupt junior

---

[9]For example, at La Bahía del Espíritu Santo in 1780, only four of the presidial troops had been born outside the Interior Provinces. See Cabello, *"Real Presidio de la Bahia de el Espíritu Santo. Extracto General de la Tropa . . .,"* January 12, 1780, San Antonio, Béxar Archives.

[10]Various land laws were in effect granting land near the presidios to the soldiers and civilians. These laws were designed not only to secure enlistments but also to encourage settlement on the frontier. The presidio of Tubac, for example, had a population of nearly 500 in 1767. Ray H. Mattison, "Early Spanish and Mexican Settlements in Arizona," *New Mexico Historical Review*, XXI (October 1946), 281-282.

[11]Lawrence Kinnaird (ed.), *The Frontiers of New Spain: Nicolas de La Fora's Description, 1766-1768* (Berkeley: The Quivira Society, 1958), 214-217; Thomas, *Teodoro de Croix*, 42.

officers. As a result they developed a defeatist attitude and reacted to orders, at best, with sullen obedience—and at times with outright insubordination. The Royal Regulations of 1772, despite the good intentions that motivated them, brought few meaningful changes in the system, leaving the frontier troops to labor under severe handicaps. Once in service, common soldiers had little time for formal instruction; their duties were too numerous. Besides defending the presidio and campaigning against Indians, the troops were used as escorts for supply trains, carried the mail, acted as guards at the missions, protected presidial horse herds, or labored on and within the forts at numerous tasks. Thus despite the fact that soldiers were enlisted for long terms—10 years —they were never given a formal course of instruction in their duties.

In 1777-1778 on his first tour of inspection of the Interior Provinces, Croix noted that all along the presidial cordon the soldiers were without competent training in handling firearms and general knowledge of military tactics.[12] Thirty years later, in 1807, Zebulon M. Pike. on his momentous trek through the Southwest commented that the soldiers he saw in the province of New Mexico would have been outstanding except for the same defects noted by Croix.[13] Without proper training or leadership, the enlisted men in the Borderlands were largely oblivious to or ignorant of their obligations. They lived secure within the solid adobe walls of their forts, drew their rations and pay, and farmed the small plots of land assigned to them. Along with the civilians, the chief concern of the soldiers was to stay alive on that bloody frontier— and, hopefully, to reach retirement age.

Disinterest in duty and officer incompetence had gone so far by 1777 that the garrison at the key post of Janos had allowed the carbines and pistols there to become rusty and unserviceable. Armed only with lances and riding inferior horses, the soldiers were virtually helpless.[14] Obviously the spirit of the Regulations of 1772 had not been enforced. Such reports were common, and they did not decrease with the passage of time. In 1817 Governor Antonio Martínez of Texas stated that soldiers under his command for the most part were barefooted, without horses, swords, or lances, and that their firearms were in such poor condition that in recent engagements only 1 out of 12 could be fired. He added that the artillery carriages were in such a state of disrepair that the cannon could not be fired, that cartridges on hand were made of worthless powder, and that there was little food and no money for the soldiers. As a result desertions were frequent, as was undisciplined behavior among the remaining men. In the meantime, Indian depredations in the province were going unpunished.[15]

---

[12]Thomas, *Teodoro de Croix*, 25.

[13]Elliott T. Coues (ed.) *The Expeditions of Zebulon M. Pike* (3 vols., New York: Francis B. Harper, 1895), II, 796-798.

[14]Thomas, *Teodoro de Croix*, 26.

[15]Virginia H. Taylor (trans. and ed.), *The Letters of Antonio Martínez* (Austin: Texas State Library, 1957), 1-87.

Improper arms were a major cause of defeat in the Interior Provinces. Because of tradition and economy the *soldados de cuera* were equipped with weapons and armament totally unsuited to the type of service in which they were engaged. Confronted with Indians who seldom fought in the open, who preferred raiding and stealing to direct armed conflict, the Spaniards needed to develop new methods of warfare. But just as the American officers who came to the frontier in the last half of the 19th century brought with them some rigid, preconceived notions about how war should be conducted, so also Spanish officers assigned to the Interior Provinces in the late 18th century came knowing only European tactics and the use of European weapons— both ill-adapted to fighting Apaches and Comanches. For example, Captain Pike, passing through New Mexico in 1807, noted that while the presidial dragoons there were probably the best horsemen in the world their methods of attack were far from effective. Assuming the enemy was massed to the front, the Spaniards relied on a direct charge to the enemy flanks, but without regularity or concert — shouting, hallooing, and firing their carbines. If, as Pike described it, the Spaniards felt themselves equal to the enemy, they charged with pistols and then lances.[16] Such an assault was in the best tradition of European warfare, but with an illusive enemy and in a broken, bushy, or mountainous country such as that in the Southwest, it was seldom successful. Such weapons and tactics varied but little with those carried and used by the soldiers of Hernán Cortéz in his conquest of Mexico more than two hundred years earlier.

Croix recognized the necessity of change and criticized the use of the long, heavy, four- to six-ply leather coats, or *cueras,* which the troops wore as protection against arrows and lances. He urged the elimination of this garment, as well as of the lance and the shield, or *adarga.* To the commandant-general it was apparent that the soldiers were armed more for defense than for offense, that the lance was retained out of tradition and because it was inexpensive. On the frontier, however, the lance was essentially a useless weapon because its effectiveness presupposed an enemy that would fight in the open, as did Europeans. The Apaches and Comanches rarely fought this way; only when cornered would they make such a stand. Encumbered by lance, shield, and *cuera,* the Spanish soldier was loath to dismount; in fact, he had not been trained to do so.[17] Nor was he quick to employ his firearms, either mounted or dismounted. He was held strictly accountable for the powder and shot he used, and was charged for any over his allotment that he expended. Consequently, he was more inclined to depend upon his lance than his flintlock.

In the opinion of Croix, troops equipped with firearms and swords and campaigning with few remounts would be far more mobile. Expe-

---

[16]Coues (ed.), *The Expeditions of Zebulon M. Pike, II,* 796-797.

[17]Thomas, *Teodoro de Croix,* 57, 152; Kinnaird, *Frontiers of New Spain,* 216.

ditions should move rapidly, and surprise attacks could be effected more often without the extra burdens that the traditional system of armament and mounting allowed. To effect this mobility the commandant-general wanted extensive use made of the *compañía volante,* or flying company, which had been introduced as early as the middle of the 17th century. Designed as a lightly armed, fast-moving unit, the flying company had proven its value for patrols and for offensive campaigns. Croix increased the number of such units in Sonora, also establishing a "Flying Corps" in Nueva Vizcaya which was made up of four companies and had a total strength of 564 men. It was not until after the turn of the 19th century, however, that presidial soldiers discarded their shields.[18]

Persuading the soldiers to abandon their lances and use their flint-locks would have been a difficult task in itself, but the problem of making such a change was compounded by a shortage of firearms on the frontier. The weapons described in the Royal Regulations of 1772 were just arriving in Sonora in the fall of 1780; but with exceptions at the presidios of Tucson and Altar, few were in use along the cordon of forts for several years thereafter— and still fewer of the men were trained to fire them.[19] The Spanish *miguelet* lock gun was an excellent weapon, well-constructed, durable, and dependable. Contemporary firearms experts believed that it was among the best flint-ignition weapons of that day, and Spanish-manufactured barrels likewise were held in high regard during the 18th century.[20] Yet a sufficient quantity of these weapons never reached the northern provinces during the Spanish period. Ammunition also was continuously in short supply; and, when it did reach the presidios, the balls sometimes would not fit the guns at the garrisons.[21] Had these new weapons been available along the presidial cordon, the ammunition supply unlimited and of the correct size, and the soldiers trained in the proper use of their guns, the frontier command doubtless would have made a more creditable showing.

Ironically, some of the Indians hostile to Spain had long been armed with French and English muskets of excellent quality, and were battle-trained in their use. French *voyageurs* had bartered weapons to the Indians of the plains as early as 1706, and by 1748 *bastante escopetas* were being sold to the Comanches along the Red River for their forays southward.[22] A few years later, English weapons were making their appearance in the hands of Indian raiders along the Spanish frontier. After 1763 and the defeat of France in North America, English weapons dominated the frontier trade. In the 1790's the partners of the North West Company, operating west and south from their headquarters in

---

[18]Thomas, *Teodoro de Croix,* 62-63.

[19]*Ibid.,* 152.

[20]Keith W. Neal, *Spanish Guns and Pistols* (London: G. Bell and Sons, 1955), 11-20; Harold L. Peterson, *The Treasury of the Gun* (New York: Golden Press, 1962), 81.

[21]Vito Allesio Robles (ed.), *Viaje de Indios y diario del Nuevo México* (Mexico City, 1935), 241.

[22]Charles F. Lummis, "A New Mexican Episode in 1748," *Land of Sunshine,* VIII (January and February 1898), 76, 126.

Montreal, played a major role in supplying the plains Indians with fire-arms. The short-barrelled "fuke," or "North West gun," became extremely popular among the nomadic tribes from Manitoba to Texas.[23] Thus the Indians had little to fear from their Spanish foes during the last years of the colonial era, despite the fact that the Spaniards had long forbidden the trade or sale of guns to them.

This ironclad Spanish policy was based in part on the scarcity of guns available for trade purposes and in part on the fear that the Indians might thus become too powerful. In 1786, however, Viceroy Bernardo de Gálvez reversed the old policy and urged that long trade guns be made available to the natives of the frontier. Incorporating this idea into an overall plan to weaken the ability of the Indians to fight, Gálvez argued that the natives should be encouraged to become dependent on firearms—and as a result they would lose their proficiency with the bow, a weapon he knew to be far more dangerous in the hands of the native than a clumsy gun. Moreover, the viceroy knew that should the Indians adopt firearms they would soon find powder and shot hard to acquire except from the Spaniards. He further pointed out that Spanish trade guns, which were of inferior quality, would continually be in a state of disrepair—and only the Spaniards could mend them. In actual practice, however, the Gálvez plan had to be modified slightly, for the natives quickly learned to judge the quality of the trade weapons and began rejecting Spanish guns. By the 1790's, therefore, the guns offered by the Spaniards to the Indians were largely of English manufacture.[24]

Despite the increase in the number of troops achieved by Croix and the changes effected in the system by him and others, little of permanent value was achieved during his tenure as commandant-general. Soon after Croix left the Interior Provinces in 1783 to become viceroy of Peru, most of his innovations were abandoned and the provincial soldiers returned to their former ways. Unable to meet the Indian enemy on the open field with any great hope of victory, the troops again cowered behind the relative security of their presidial walls. High Spanish officials were soon forced to a policy of conciliation, of buying peace through annual distributions of presents of such value that the Indians would prize peace more than war. The Indians were induced where possible to settle near the presidios in what came to be known as *estable-cimientos de paz* — establishments of peace. Thus the Apaches and the Comanches were never permanently defeated by the *soldados de cuera;*

---

[23]Carl Russell, *Guns on the Early Frontier* (Berkeley and Los Angeles: University of California Press, 1957), 33-37, 108-109; Herbert E. Bolton, *Athanase de Mézières and the Louisiana-Texas Frontier, 1768-1780* (2 vols., Cleveland: The Arthur H. Clark Company, 1914), I, 68, 76-79; Thomas, *The Plains Indians*, 161-164.

[24]Russell, *Guns on the Early Frontier*, 37; Bernardo de Gálvez, *Instructions for Governing the Interior Provinces of New Spain, 1786*, trans. and ed. by Donald E. Worcester (Berkeley: The Quivíra Society, 1951), 83.

they were neutralized only by gifts.[25] When the War for Independence began in Mexico in 1810 and the distribution of presents stopped, the savages took to the warpath again in increased numbers, thundering past the useless defense cordon of presidios into the interior of Mexico.[26]

Despite the many weaknesses of the Spanish system, the Interior Provinces were still a part of the Empire until the end of the Mexican Revolution. The borderlands from Texas to Sonora had not been totally depopulated by Indian raids, nor had the area been wrested from the Spanish grip by French, English, or American filibusters who coveted it. Considering the shortage of supplies and funds, the paucity of support from higher echelons of government, the poor training of the soldiers, and the barbaric ferocity of the natives, the wonder is not that the Spaniards largely failed in their military objectives but that they succeeded as well as they did.

---

[25]H. H. Bancroft, *History of Arizona and New Mexico* (San Francisco: The History Company, 1889), 378-379; H. H. Bancroft, *History of the North Mexican States and Texas* (2 vols., San Francisco: The History Company, 1884), I, 594-595; Gomez Pedraza, *Decree Establishing and Organizing Presidios for the Defense of the Northern Territories* (Mexico City, 1826).

Few of the treaties made with Indian bands during the late colonial period were a result of military victories. One of the exceptions was Anza's military successes against the western Comanches in New Mexico beginning in 1779. Faced with continued defeats, the Comanches sought peace, and in 1786 a treaty of alliance was signed. The peace lasted for nearly 20 years. However, the Spaniards were less successful against the Navajos in New Mexico. Isolated bands were defeated, but no permanent peace with this tribe was secured during the Spanish period. Thomas, *Forgotten Frontiers,* 83.

[26]The Indian problem after 1810 was particularly serious in Texas, New Mexico and Sonora. Alliances with the various Indian tribes fell apart during the confusion of the Mexican war for Independence, and the troops often could not retaliate even against minor thefts. In Arizona the relative peace apparently continued for a longer period. As late as 1819 several previously hostile Apache bands requested permission to settle at Tucson, and Arizona was not seriously threatened again until 1831 when the Apaches attacked in large numbers. Thomas, *Forgotten Frontiers,* 83. Documents 6191 and 6206 in Charles E. Chapman, *Catalogue of Materials in the Archivo General de Indias* (Berkeley: University of California Press, 1919), 718, 719.

APPENDIX A

Presidios of the Frontier Line
Listed in the Royal Regulations

[In order mentioned in the Regulation; also see map opposite page 80]

SANTA GERTRUDIS DEL ALTAR, designed to restrain the Seris, Pimas and
   Papagos. Lawrence Kinnaird, *The Frontiers of New Spain*,
   (Berkeley: The Quivíra Society, 1958), 112. Founded in 1755 by
   Captain Bernardo de Urrea with 30 soldiers from the presidio of
   Sinaloa. Called Santa Gertrudis del Altar and then Nuestra
   Señora de Guadalupe del Altar. Francisco R. Almada, *Diccion-
   ario de Historia, Geografía, y Biografía Sonorenses* (Chihua-
   hua: n.p., n.d.), 55.

TUBAC, founded in 1753 following the disastrous Pima uprising of 1751.
   The garrison was moved to Tucson in 1777 upon the orders of
   the commandant-inspector, Hugo O'Conor. Later the presidio
   was regarrisoned by Pima Indian auxiliaries. Tubac guarded
   the missions of present-day Arizona. Because it was vulnerable
   to Indian attack, O'Conor planned to move the presidio to El
   Arivac, the present hamlet of Arivaca, Arizona. The move was
   never made. H. H. Bancroft, *History of Arizona and New Mexico* (San Francisco: The History Company, 1889), 369.

TERRENATE, founded in 1742 southwest of the Huachuca Mountains
   in Sonora. In 1775 the presidial garrison was moved two
   leagues southeasterly to the arroyo of Las Nutrias as ordered by
   the Royal Regulations. The new location was such a short distance from the original site, Don Hugo O'Conor determined
   that the presidio should be moved northward. Late in 1775 the
   troops were sent down the San Pedro River to a location formerly
   known as Quiburi. Here on the west bank of the river, near present Fairbank, Arizona, a presidio was built and settlers brought
   to establish farms. The new settlement was known as Santa Cruz
   de Terrenate. Apache Indian attacks became so violent there in
   the late 1770's, however, that Don Teodoro de Croix ordered the

site abandoned. In 1780 Terrenate was relocated near the arroyo of Las Nutrias. It appears that a few soldiers remained at the San Pedro site as late as 1788. Almada, *Diccionario,* 758. Bancroft, *History of Arizona and New Mexico,* 362. A. B. Thomas, *Teodoro de Croix and the Northern Frontier of New Spain, 1776-1783* (Norman: University of Oklahoma Press, 1941), 181-204. Charles C. DiPeso, *The Sobaipuri Indians of the Upper San Pedro Valley, Southeastern Arizona* (Dragoon, Arizona: The Amerind Foundation, Inc., 1953), 42-48.

FRONTERAS, founded in 1692 by Captain Francisco Ramirez de Salazar; known then as Santa Rosa de Corodehuachi; afterward designated Presidio de las Fronteras de los Apaches. Almada, *Diccionario,* 282. It was for a while located to the north in the San Bernardino Valley, possibly in Arizona, then was moved south by Croix, about 1780, to its final location as shown on the map opposite page 80. Thomas, *Teodoro de Croix,* 51.

JANOS, founded in 1690. Kinnaird, *Frontiers of New Spain,* 14.

SAN BUENAVENTURA, founded in 1776 by troops from Guajoquilla. Kinnaird, *Frontiers of New Spain,* 9.

EL PASO DEL NORTE. As a result of the Revolt of 1680 in upper New Mexico, the Spaniards moved downriver (southward) and founded El Paso, at the site of present Juarez, Chihuahua. The presidio was built in 1683. Nearby several missions were built by the Franciscans, even as far south as La Junta, present Presidio, Texas. In 1773, because the town of El Paso was well populated and could defend itself, the presidio was moved southward to Carrizal. Kinnaird, *Frontiers of New Spain* 13-14. Thomas, *Teodoro de Croix,* 39.

GUAJOQUILLA, erected at the orders of Viceroy Revilla Gigedo in 1752. Later known as San Eleazario. Kinnaird, *Frontiers of New Spain,* 9.

JULIMES, located in 1777 at the former site of the presidio of La Junta at the confluence of the Conchos and Del Norte (Rio Grande) rivers. Thomas, *Teodoro de Croix,* 24.

CERRO GORDO, also known as San Carlos de Cerro Gordo. This presidio was founded after 1772 as part of the new frontier defense, and was named after an abandoned presidio 240 miles to the south. Kinnaird, *Frontiers of New Spain,* 38, 63.

SAN SABÁ, often referred to as Aguaverde, the name San Sabá was given to the location after the abandonment of a presidio of the same name in Texas in 1768. San Sabá-Aguaverde was founded in the new presidial line after 1772. Kinnaird, *Frontiers of New Spain,* 38.

SANTA ROSA DEL SACRAMENT, now Cuidad Melchor Muzquiz, Coahuila. Moved north after 1772, the original location in the Santa Rosa Valley was abandoned as a military post. After 1780 the presidio of La Babia protected the Santa Rosa Valley. Thomas, *Teodoro de Croix*, 50, 54. In 1780 Croix recommended that San Carlos, San Sabá, and La Bahía should be moved or abandoned because of their poor locations. No action was taken. Thomas, *Teodoro de Croix*, 49-50.

MONCLOVA, founded in 1674 by Antonio de Balcarel. Walter Prescott Webb, *Handbook of Texas* (Austin: Texas State Historical Association, 1952), II, 221. The villa or town of Monclova was the capital of Coahuila in 1780. At that time the presidio was located to the east, nearer the Rio Grande. Thomas, *Teodoro de Croix*, 36.

SAN JUAN BAUTISTA, founded in 1699. Bancroft, *North Mexican States and Texas*, I, 379.

LA BAHÍA DEL ESPÍRITU SANTO. The last and easternmost presidio of the line, actually named Nuestra Señora de Loreto. Founded in 1772 at the orders of the Marquis de Aguayo. Original site where Fort St. Louis stood on Matagorda Bay. Moved in 1726 to the Guadalupe River, and in 1749 removed to the north bank of the San Antonio River at the site of the present town of Goliad, Texas. Webb, *Handbook of Texas*, II, 2.

SAN ANTONIO DE BÉJAR. This defended settlement was founded on May 5, 1718, by Martín de Alarcón. Webb, *Handbook*, II, 541.

ARROYO DEL CÍBOLO, a detachment site founded on April 12, 1771, by Gov. Baron de Ripperdá, of Texas. Located at the Tawakoni Crossing on Cíbolo Creek between San Antonio and La Bahía. Deactivated in 1782 at orders of Teodoro de Croix. Odie B. Faulk, *The Last Years of Spanish Texas* (The Hague: Mouton & Co., 1964), 39.

Additional presidios were garrisoned in the 1780's behind the frontier cordon. Most of these were not considered as part of the frontier defense, but as protection against internal Indian uprisings. The presidio of Tucson (San Agustín del Tucson) had been established in 1776 north of the presidial cordon in order to protect the route to the Colorado River and California, and to defend the pueblo of Tucson as well as nearby Mission of San Xavier del Bac.

Publication History of the Royal Regulations of 1772

Prior to the issuance of the presidial regulations of 1772, the Spanish government of New Spain had made only one significant attempt to standardize the operations of the few presidios on the northern frontier. In 1729, the viceroy, Juan de Acuña de Casa-Fuerte, ordered published a series of military regulations for the management of frontier presidios. These regulations were based on the report of Brigadier D. Pedro de Rívera, who spent four years surveying the military establishments of the interior provinces. While these regulations were not as detailed as those that followed, with modifications they served until 1772.

There are eight known printings of the Regulations of 1772, five of them Spanish imprints and the remaining three published in the Republic of Mexico. The editions vary in length from 30 pages to 132 pages. The difference is explained by the fact that page and type sizes varied greatly from one edition to another, and because some editions contain a considerable body of introductory material that in essence was not part of the Regulations but an explanation of conditions in New Spain which led to their formulation. The text of the regulations themselves, beginning with the pronouncement introduced in the classic style, *El Rey,* is identical in all editions, even after Mexico had achieved independence from Spain.

The first known publication of the regulations was on July 18, 1771, under authority of El Marqués de Croix, Viceroy of New Spain. This set of 55 orders, released some months in advance of the king's official acceptance of the regulations, was to take effect on January 1, 1772, and remain in force until the arrival of the new royal regulations from Spain. Following a *cedula,* or order by King Charles III on September 10, 1772, the regulations were printed in Madrid and sent to Mexico. Soon after that first printing in Spain, in 1773 a reprint was produced in Mexico City. The last known Spanish printing was in 1822 in Madrid. An edition printed in the early 1820's on the northern frontier was probably completed after Mexico had won its independence. Mexican reprints also were produced in 1827 and 1834.

Faced with the problem of controlling Indian enemies inherited from Spain, the Mexican government chose to continue the frontier defense system set up in the 1772 regulations. The republican government modified the uniforms, purchased new types of firearms, and made some changes in presidio locations, but until nearly 1850 the original system remained largely in force.

It is presumed that a copy of the regulations was available at each presidio of the Interior Provinces (or *Provincias Internas*), and that there were other copies for officials at Mexico City and Guadalajara. A detailed bibliographical listing of these various editions may be found in Henry R. Wagner, *The Spanish Southwest 1542-1794,* II. (Albuquerque: The Quivíra Society, 1937.)

The 1834 edition was selected for use in LANCERS FOR THE KING because the type style, page size, and legibility of this printing were most adaptable to reproduction.

Facsimiles Of Documents
Used By The Authors

This section includes a selection of documents which are typical of the many utilized by the authors in their study. All have been reproduced from microfilm holdings of the incomparable Bancroft Library at the University of California, which acquired this material over an extended period of time from the Archives of the Indies at Seville, Spain. That faraway depository of Spanish Colonial records is the fountainhead of research into Hispanic history. Its directors and curators have been generously co-operative with scholars from the New World in opening the records of the Spanish empire to citizens of its strongest successor in the Western hemisphere. The scope and wealth of the Archives was revealed to Americans a half-century ago when a succession of Fellows supported by the Native Sons of the Golden West, many being students of the late Prof. Herbert Eugene Bolton, spent laborious months and years carefully unrolling the old documents and calendaring them for analysis and translation. An outstanding bibliographical resource for the Archives of the Indies is a work resulting from that investigative period: *Catalogue of Materials in the Archivo General de Indias for the History of the Pacific Coast and the American Southwest*. The compiler was Dr. Charles E. Chapman, the work being published in 1919 by the University of California Press. Dr. Chapman listed 6,257 documents, reports, and studies with a bearing upon Southwestern history, noting that he had passed over countless others that had less direct bearing upon his interest in the Greater Southwest. These included numerous secondary documents that contain minute detail of the operations of military establishments in Nueva Vizcaya. The Bancroft Library film includes items that for one reason or another Dr. Chapman did not list.

With the exception of the first, the documents reproduced in facsimile are arranged in chronological order.

[1]   Although Carlos III [*see portrait frontispiece*] was, by the Grace of God, the King of Castile and of many lands and possessions in two hemispheres, and held numerous other royal titles, the printer of this form of royal commission for military captains did not see fit to include Nueva Vizcaya among Carlos' titles and honors "too numerous to mention." This was the commission of a captain of the Third Company of the First Squadron of Dragoons in the province of Nueva Vizcaya, conferred on March 1, 1782.

[2]   Letter from Captain Mateo Sastre of the presidio of San Miguel de Horcasitas to Viceroy Antonio Bucareli y Ursua. Sastre opposed a project to invade the Apache country, arguing that the presidial troops were not even able to defend their own territory, indeed that they were not safe "by the light of the midday sun in their own homes." The Spanish government insisted upon meticulous record keeping. This is Copy No. 2 of the original, "copied to the letter" by one of the scribes who found ample and often rewarding employment in the New World.

[3]   Extract of a review and inspection made by Colonel Hugo O'Conor at the presidio of San Ignacio de Tubac in 1775. Such reviews were a regular part of O'Conor's duties as Commandant-Inspector of the Interior Provinces between 1772 and 1776. At the front of such reports was usually placed a summary so that O'Conor's superiors could quickly evaluate the strength of each presidio. Note that at Tubac, the only Spanish outpost in Arizona in 1775, there were only three officers and fifty-two soldiers.

[4]   Report of a campaign made in Sonora and Nueva Vizcaya against the Apaches in July of 1777. Captain Francisco Trespalacios from the presidio of Terrenate and Captain Juan Bautista Perú of Janos led 150 troops to the village of the Mimbres Apaches and succeeded in killing three Indians on one occasion and four on another. The report was written at Durango a few months later.

[5]   Review of inspection at San Agustín del Tucson made by the Assistant Inspector Roque de Medina in May of 1779. The last sheet is a fitness report on the captain of the presidio, Captain Pedro de Allande Sabedra.

Born in 1741 Allande had entered the Spanish army at the age of 13 as a cadet; had served in the infantry of Navarre, the cavalry of Malta, the royal guards, and the dragoons of Mexico; and had fought in various engagements in Europe. Inspector Medina noted that Captain Allande was occasionally inclined to assign "cruel and improper punishments to his troops," but that he maintained "good subordination and discipline." Next is an inventory or listing of arms and armament at Tucson: 16 muskets, 48 lances, 78 swords, and 4 bronze cannon. The latter probably were the four-pounders which had been transferred from Tubac.

[6]   A resume of the deaths and robberies noted in the Interior Provinces during the last four months of 1779. The report, signed by Commandant-General Teodoro de Croix, shows that 102 Indians had been killed and 46 taken prisoner. This heavy toll was largely the result of a successful campaign of Colonel Juan Bautista de Anza in New Mexico. [The word "*Ydem*" was the Spanish equivalent of "*ditto*."]

[7]   Copies of letters relating to the surrender at Tucson on May 13, 1819 of Chilitipagé, chief of an Apache tribe. Ten other sub-chiefs joined him at that presidio, requesting to be allowed to settle peacefully in *establecimientos de paz*. These letters are especially noteworthy because of the late date of the request—1819. The first letter indicates that Chilitipagé's band comprised 236 souls.

[1]

✠

DON CARLOS , POR LA GRACIA DE DIOS , REY DE CASTILLA, de Leon, de Aragón, de las dos Sicilias, de Jerusalén, de Navarra, de Granada, de Toledo, de Valencia, de Galicia, de Mallorca, de Sevilla, de Cerdeña, de Cordova, de Corcega, de Murcia, de Jaén, de los Algarves, de Algecira, de Gibraltár, de las Islas de Canaria, de las Indias Orientales, y Occidentales, Islas, y Tierra firme del Mar Occeano, Archiduque de Austria, Duque de Borgoña, de Brabante, y Milán, Conde de Abspurg, de Flandes, Tiról, y Barcelona, Señor de Bizcaya, y de Molina, &c. Por quanto *en atencion a los meritos y servicios de vos D. Juan Egidio del Valle, he venido en conferiros el empleo de Capitan de la tercera Compañia del primer Escuadron del Cuerpo de Dragones Provinz.^s de Sn Juan Bautista Milicias de la Nueva Vizcaya, vacante p.^r muerte de D. Valeriano Gamiz*

Por tanto mándo al *Comand.^e Genl de las Provin.^s Internas de Nueva España* dé la orden conveniente para que se os ponga en posesion de la referida Compañia, y à los Oficiales , y Soldados de ella, que os reconozcan, y respeten por su Capitan, obedeciendo las Ordenes que les diereis de mi Servicio, por escrito, y de palabra, sin réplica, ni dilacion alguna ; y que asi ellos, como los demas Cabos mayores, y menores, Oficiales, y Soldados de mis Exercitos, os hayan, y tengan por tal Capitan de *l refer.^do Cuerpo* de Milicias, guardandoos, y haciendoos guardar las honras, preeminencias, y exempciones, que os tocan, y deben ser guardadas, sin que os falte cosa alguna, que asi es mi voluntad ; y que el *d.^ho Comand.^e Genl de las refer.^s Provincias Internas* dé asimismo la orden necesaria, para que en los Oficios principales de mi Real Hacienda se tome razon de este Despacho, y se os forme asiento ; con prevencion, de que siempre que mande juntar *el mencion.^o Cuerpo* para acudir à los parages que convenga à mi Real Servicio, se os asistirá con el sueldo, que à los demas Capitanes de *Dragones* de Tropas regladas, en consecuencia de lo que tengo resuelto. Dado en *el Pardo* à *primero* de *Marzo* de mil setecientos *ochenta y dos.*

Yo el Rey ✠

Patente de Capitan *de la tercera Comp.^a del primer Escuadron de Dragones Provinz.^s de Sn Juan Bautista a D. Juan Egidio del Valle.*

[2]

Copia N° 2°

Ilmo Señor_ Señor_ Nunca menos que aora

conviene salga tropa alguna a hacer correría

a la Apacheria, y solo si el que se mantenga

en los parages que he establecido el Destacamento

de observación que formé en el Campo de san

Bernardino, frontera de esta a Chihuahua, por

que Señor, si no podemos defender nuestra misma

Casa con toda la pequeña fuerza de la tropa,

menos lo haremos si esta esta campeando,

y abandona el Presidio que guarnece: Prueba

de ello que en el dia diez y siete de octubre

a las doce de el atacaron los Barbaros

la Cauallada del Presidio de Tubac al cargo

de D. Juan Baptista de Ansa, y le llebaron

Ciento, y mas Cauallos, segun he sado parte

a V.E. anteriormente; y el dia quince de Dici-

embre antecedente a D. José Antonio de Vildo

sola en Terrenate se le llebaron docientos se_

[103]

[2]

semeas quatro Cauallos. Con que Señor, si esto sucede à la luz del Sol al medio dia en sus mismas Casas, no se'como hay valor de solicitar Empresas semejantes, pues si es el animo buscarlos, y escarmentarlos sin la pena de irlos à buscar alli los tienen, pues no se esconden yendolos arrisar muy de dia. Todo esto ha consistido en no hauerme obedecido en punto à que incesantemente corriesen las Patrullas por las avenidas de los Enemigos à una no larga distancia de cada Presidio para que al aviso que diesen con anticipación à su llegada, pudiera disponerse toda la Guarnicion, y recivir à los Barbaros con espada en mano como lo executa una Gran-Guardia de Cavalleria, à cuya parte se bate (si es menester) la General en un Exercito, poniendose la Tropa sobre las Armas, precaucion que asegura à esta suna,

[2]

sorpresa. Nada acredita mas la importancia de la practica de esta disposicion mia, como el no haver sorprendido, ni llevado Cavallada alguna de la Tropa de este Presidio donde existo, ni el Altar à cargo de D. Bernardo Urrea ni el de Fronteras al de D. Gabriel de Vildosola, porque aqui, y alli se practicò puntualmente, con lo que satisfago à la Carta de Vé. con fecha de trece de Octubre en que se digna remitirme copia de la Representacion de D. Juan Baptista de Ansa. Nuestro Señor que la Persona de Vé. m.a como necesito Real Presidio de San Miguel de Orcasitas, y Enero 21 de 1773. Exmo señor = B. L. M. de V. E. su mas reverente Criado Mateo Sastre—

Exmo S. fr D. Ant.º Maria Bucareli y Ursua.

Es copia à la letra de su original que queda en la Secretaria de Camara del Virreynato que es à mi cargo de que certifico. Mexico veintey seis de Abril de mil setecientos setentay tres.—

Melchor de Peramas

[3]

Prov.ª de Sonóra.

Año

de

1775.

Extracto de Revista de Inspeccion.

pasada por el Coronel de Infanteria.

Dr. Hugo Oconór

Comandante Inspector de todos los Presidios

~ internos de Nueba Esp.ª

al expresado de 8.ª Ygnacio

de~

Tubác.

Quad.º n.º 1.º

[3]

Presidiales de la Provin.ᵃ de Sonora	Cavalleria	Real Presidio de TUBAC, mes. ᵉ Ag.ᵗᵒ de 1775.

Extracto de la Revista de Inspeccion executada por mi D.ⁿ Hugo Oconór, Cav.ᵒ el Ordⁿ ᵈᵉ Calatrava, Coronel de Infanteria de los R.ˢ Exercitos, y Comandante Inspector ᵈᵉ todos los Presidios internos de esta N.ᵃ E. en nueve ᵈᵉ Agosto ᵈᵉ mil setecientos setenta y cinco, à la Comp.ᵃ de Cavalleria q.ᵉ guarnece dho R.ˡ Presidio ~ ~ ~

	Compañia.	Hombs.	Cavallos	Mulas.
Cap.ⁿ graduado Ret.ᵈᵒ Col. D.ⁿ Juan Bapᵗᵃ ᵈᵉ Anza, Comisᵈᵒ en Monᵗᵉ-Rey: como Capᵗ ____ **CP**...1	Sargᵗ Vacᵗᵉ ____	V.	0	0...
	Cabos, pᵗᵃ dos ____	P....2.	13	2...
Thent.ᵉ D.ⁿ Juan Maria ᵈᵉ Oliva, pxesᵗᵉ ____ P...1.	Soldados pᵗ guarⁿ ____	P...40.	167	27...
Alferez D.ⁿ Felipe Beldexxain, pxᵗᵉ ____ P...1	Indios Exploradores pxesᵗᵉ diez ____	P...10.	29.	5...
Capellan Vacᵗᵃ ____ **V**				
	Totales.	52	229	34

Nota

Esta Compañia rebajado un despedido por sus defectos, y accidentes habituales, como manifiesta la relacion n.5. queda en la fuerza efectiva ᵈᵉ cincuenta y dos Plazas incluso el Sargento que se hallaba vacante en el acto ᵈᵉ la Revista, y que despues ᵈᵉ ella se proveyò en Pedro Marques Sargento que fue ᵈᵉ la Compañia volante ᵈᵉ Sonora ____

La calidad ᵈᵉ esta Gente consiste en un Capitan Criollo, un Theniente Español un Alferez idem, dos Cavos Españoles, diez y seis Soldados idm, quince Coyotes, ocho Mulatos, un Mestizo, y diez Indios exploradores de la Nacion Opata ____

La talla ᵈᵉ esta tropa, es inferior, como asimismo su disposicion, aptitud, Robustez, y aunque diestros en manejarse à Cavallo, carecen de los primeros rudimentos ᵈᵉ la disciplina Militar, y metodo regular ᵈᵉl servicio; reduciendose el que hazen à solamente guardia ᵈᵉ Quartel, y Cavallada: y aunque ay noticias ciertas de introducirse à la Provincia algunos enemigos, no se incomoda esta tropa en seguirlos, quexandose de estos procedimientos, y con sobrados fundamentos los Moradores del Pays, por el ningun abrigo que hasta aora han hallado en las armas ᵈᵉ esta Provincia ____

De las cuentas seguidas à los Individuos ᵈᵉ esta Compañia por el Havilitado de ella el Alferez D.ⁿ Juan Felipe Beldexxain desde el dia 1.º ᵈᵉ Junio ᵈᵉl año pasado de 1774 en que se ha puesto, resultan alcanzando algunos Individuos ᵈᵉ ella setecientos diez pesos, cinco ᵗˢ quatro gˢ los mismos que hize entregar à los Interesados, y con arreglo à lo prevenido en el art.º 3. titᵘˡᵒ 6 ᵈᵉ la R.ˡ instruccion, como asimismo al Comandante ᵈᵉ la Comp.ᵃ la correspondiente advertencia para el descuento ᵈᵉ los quinientos nueve pesos siete ᵗˢ cinco granˢ que quedaron debiendo siete Soldados ᵈᵉ la Comp.ᵃ, y los diez Indios Exploradores al Havilitado, hasta el citado dia treinta de Junio proxᵒ anterior, como acredita la relacion n.º 7, y mis providencias dictadas en el art.º 47 de la carta resolutiva N.º 13 ____

Toda la tropa se ha quexado con sobrados fundamentos, ᵈᵉ la conducta ᵈᵉ su Havilitado, quien ha sabido comprar los efectos à unos precios, y entregarlos à los Soldados à otros mayores, cuyo hecho se ha justificado plenamente en la confrontaᵉⁱᵒn qᵉ hize de las cuentas; y por el mismo considero conduzente, al mejor servicio ᵈᵉl Rey, el q.ᵉ à por la superioridad ᵈᵉ separe à este Oficial del R.ˡ servicio, imponi-

[3]

...dole la pena correspondiente á su indigno proceder, y para que sirva de
exemplar á otros.————

Quedan depositados en la Caxa de gratificacion de diez pesos por plaza, los
quatrocientos p.s q.e le corresponden hasta fin de Junio proximo venidero, por haver
hecho devoluciesen á ella las descuentos que manifiesta la relacion N.o 10. Y asi mismo setecientos diez pesos relativos al fondo de veinte p.s por plaza como acredita
la relacion N.o 11.

El Vestuario de esta Comp.a se halla enteramente inutil, y todos sus Individuos
quasi en cueros, y para que con la maior posible brevedad se ponga en estado,
previniendola sean completo Vestuario, hize al Comandante las advertencias cons-
tantes en los articulos 2. 3. 4. y 5. de la carta resolutiva N.o 13.————

Componese el armamento de algunas aunque pocas escopetas Barzelonesas
de mediano servicio, y las demás casi inutiles de las Fabricas del Reyno, y de distintos
y cortos calibres. Las lanzas y espadas desiguales en sus tamaños: pero he mandado no se proceda á su composicion y si á su entero nuevo con la brevedad posible, respecto á que debe venir de Mexico un nuebo armamento para los Presidios
de esta Provincia como acredita el articulo 16 de la carta resolutiva N.o 13.————

La Cavallada de este Presidio se halla en mediano estado, y he dispuesto el rem-
plazo de sesenta y nuebe cavallos, y catorce mulas que para el completo de los 7 que
debe tener cada uno faltan á los Soldados expresados en el art.o 7 de la referida carta resolutiva N.o 13.————

Toda la Montura de que usa esta Comp.a está en estado de servicio á excepcion de
los estrivos de palo q.e son abiertos y debiendo ser cerrados como previene el art.o 7.
tit.o 4 de la Real instruccion, he mandado se provea immediatamente de los que
previene el citado art.o use esta tropa como acredita el 6. de la carta resolutiva N.o 13.

Haviendo notado algunas confusiones en el libro de Filiaciones de este Presidio, y
para evitarlas en lo venidero pasé al Coman.te del los años y formularios que
manifiestan los articulos 23-24. y 25. y 26. de la carta Resolutiva N.o 13. y para las cuentas giñales de Cargo y Data que ha de llevar el Havilitado de esta Comp.a y la particular de cada uno de los Individuos de que se compone y de que se lleven las
advertencias y formulario que manifiestan los art.s 9. 40. 11. 42. 13. 14. 15. y 16 de la
carta resolutiva N.o 13.————

Estan aionadas á la Real Hab.ta las bajas ocurridas en esta Compañia desde el dia primero de Junio del año pasado de mil setecientos setenta y quatro hasta
treinta de Junio del corriente.————

Se debe de esta Comp.a la polvora correspondiente desde primero de Enero de mil
setecientos setenta y quatro.————

Respecto á hallarse ausente el Capitan de este Presidio d.n Juan Bap.ta de Anssa, y tener en su poder los Despachos que obtubo para este empleo, no se pueden citar en
este extracto.————

El Theniente d.n Juan Mexia de Oliva sirve desde prim.o de Abril de mil setecientos
cincuenta y quatro digo cincuenta y dos en calidad de Sargento de le ascendió á Alferez,
en cinco de Abril de mil setecientos cinquenta y quatro, y en siete de Julio de mil setecientos cincuenta y ocho á su actual empleo por nombram.o de su Capitan. Es bizarro Oficial, de valor, y buena conducta, pero no sabe leer ni escribir. Ha recivido onze heridas de los enemigos, en varios encuentros que se le han ofrecido, y es digno de q.e S. M.
le conceda el retiro con el sueldo de Inválidos p.a alivio, y descanso de sus fatigas.

El Alferez d.n Felipe Belderrain, lo es en virtud de nombram.te de su Capitan desde onze de Junio del año pasado de mil setecien.s sesenta y uno, quien á mas de su mala conducta, y pusilanimidad, tiene otros muchos vicios que le hazen acreedor á su total
separacion del Real serv.o————

En el año de mil setecientos cinquenta y tres fué exigido este Presidio en la Frontera de la Pimeria alta, y Parage n.o Tubac con motivo del alzamiento de los Pimas.

El estado N.o 12 manifiesta el de las armas, municiones, pertrechos, y utiles que
correspondientes á S. M. se guardan en este Presidio.————

El Vezindario agregado á este Presidio se compone de quarenta y una Familias
de Razon: dos de Indios de la Nacion Opata: una de la de Rixos: y otras de Apaches; pero
todos tan desdichados que no se puede contar con ellos p.a su subsistencia en este Pueblo
una vez trasladada la Tropa á su nuevo destino del Tucson, y que es regular
sigan á esta por ser los Individuos de ella, sus Hijos, Sobrinos, hermanos, y parientes
tan immediatos que se inclinan segun me insinuaron, á pasarse al nuebo Presidio.
= R.l Presidio de Tubac 18. de Agosto de 1775 = d.n Hugo Oconor————

[4]

Extracto de las principales operaciones executadas~ por los Destacamentos de las Provincias de Sonora y Nueva Vizcaya que compuestos cada uno de ciento, y cincuenta Hombres salieron à Campaña contra los Apaches del Gila en el Mes de Julio proximo pasado bajo las Ordenes de los Capitanes de Terrenate D.n Francisco Ygnacio Trespalacios, y D.n Juan Perù el de Janos.

A llegar iva D.n Juan Bautista Pe-rù con el Destacamento de su cargo à la Pla-ya que nombran de Santo Domingo quan-do encontrò con el de la Sonora, y su Co-mandante D.n Francisco Trespalacios habia yà atacado una Ranchería sin apresar Ganado alguno, y si treinta y ocho Cavallos que tenían los Enemigos.

El Capitan volante D.n Fran.co Me-nocal siguiò dos rastros frescos, y sentido nu-estro Campo de los Apaches se avisaron con humos.

En vista de esto deter-

[4]

minó Perú, con acuerdo de todos los Oficiales,
volverse al Presidio de Janos, dando à
entender à los Barbaros que ya se retira
va de sus tierras.

Hizolo así, y marchando nuevam.^{te}
à la Sierra de los Mimbres destacó un
Subalterno con cincuenta Hombres à que re
conociese la de la Florida, con lo que se logró
la muerte de tres Indios, mas Perú cercó el
dia 20. de Julio la citada Sierra de los
Mimbres, y sorprendió una Ranchería
de veinte Gandules, de los quales murieron
quatro, huyeron los demás, se apresaron
seis Piezas, la mayor de diez y seis Años,
se restauró un Cautivo, y se quitaron do
ze Bestias, y algunos Fuetes.

Durango 33. de Octubre de 1777

[5]

Provincia
de Sora ⟩

· Año de 1779

R.ᵇ Presidio de S.ⁿ
Agustin del Tucson

Revista passada por el Ayudante Inspector
D.ⁿ Roque de Medina à la compañia de Cavalleria
que guarnece el expresado
Presidio

Guadalajara 277

ARCHIVO GENERAL DE INDIAS SEVILLA

[5]

El Capitan D.ᵉ Pedro de *Allanez Sabedra* su edad 3ᵉ años, su Pais *Villa de Ponevedra* su calidad *Noble* su salud *buena* sus servicios y circunstancias que expresa.

Tiempo en que empezó á servir los Empleos.				Tiempo q ha que sirve, y quanto en cada Empleo.			
Empleos.	Dias.	Meses.	Años.	Empleos.	Años.	Meses.	Dias.
Cad.ᵗᵉ d. Inf.ᵃ de Navarra	28	Julio	1754	Cadete	4	10	6
2.ᵈᵒ en el de Cav.ᵃ d Malta	10	Junio	1759	Idem	0	7	11
Guard.ᵃ de Corp.ˢ de la Comp.ᵃ Española	18	Marzo	1760	Guard.ᵃ de Corps	4	2	12
Then.ᵗᵉ de Drag.ˢ d.l Rexi miento d Mex.ᵒ	37	Maio	1764	Theniente	12	8	18
Cap.ᵗ d.l 2.ᵈ Reg.ᵗᵒ d.l ... g.ᵒ de Julac	17	Febrero	1771	Capitan	7	10	11
Total hasta fin de *Diciembre d 1778*					24	8	4

Regimientos donde ha servido.

E.ᵗᵒ de Infanteria de Navarra, Malta de Cavalleria, Guardia de Corps, y Dragones de Mexico.

Campañas, y acciones de Guerra en que se ha hallado.

En la Guerra de Portugal el año de 1762. En la expedicion d Sonora desde el año de 176... el de 77, en cuia Guerra ataco varias veces á los Enemigos, logrando algunas funciones en las q murieron varios Barbaros, y escogieron hacer prisioneros muchas de sus familias; como asi mismo en Ceuta salió al Campo del Moro, muchas ocaciones, y salió al socorro de las Embarcac.ᵐᵒ mas q se perdieron en la Costa Enemiga el año d 1756.

Pedro de Allanez Sabedra [signature]

Informe del Inspector.	Notas de l Capitan
Este capitan es d genio recio el que le motiva á dar á su tropa algunos castigos crueles é impropios; la que tiene vien subordinada y diciplinada, en lo que ha procurado dar cumplimiento a su obligacion. *Medina* [signature]	Valor. . . la tiene Aplicacion. . . ... Capacidad. . . buena Conducta. . . ... Estado. . . Bueno *Allanez* [signature]

[5]

Real Presidio de San Agustin del Tucson   N.º 10

Relacion del Armamento de Repuesto que consta en este Presidio en el dia de mi
entrega, y del que se recivio del Justicia de Tubac, D.ⁿ Juan Ramirez con expresion
del que se ha Distribuido, y el que existe.

Escopetas Ripoleñas

Se Recivieron...........	„ „	16

Distribucion

Se han Repartido a la Tropa...........	„	5.
existen...........	„	11
Total	16.	„ „ 16
	Ygual.....	„ 0

Lanzas con casquillos

Recividas...........		48.

Distribucion

Repartidas en la Tropa...........	„ „	9.
En poder del Capitan...........	„ „	2
existen...........	„	37
Total 48...........	„ „	48
	Ygual.....	„ 0

Lanzas de Lengueta se recivieron y existen........... „ „ 12

Espadas

se recivieron...........		24 „
Repartidas en la Tropa...........	„	15
existen...........	„	9
Total 24.		24
	Ygual.....	0

Balas de cañon con el peso,
de 4. libras cada vna

Se recivieron...........		78 „
consumidas en Balas de fusil...........	„	12.
existen...........	„	66 „
Total 78. „	„	78 „
	Ygual.....	„ 0

Se recivieron, y existen quatro Cañones de Bronce........... „ 4 „
Vn Rollo de Mechas........... „ 1 „

[5]

Dos Sacatrapos existen 2,,

Tres atacadores 3,

Presidio de San Agustin del Tucson 3 de Mayo de 1779,

Roque de Medina

Guadalajara 277

[6]

Resumen de las muertes y robos que han ocurrido en las Provincias Ynternas de Nueva España en los quatro meses ultimos del año de 1779.

Provincias.	Agresores.	Españoles muertos.	Ydem Cautiv.	Enemigos muertos.	Ydem Cautiv.	Bestias robadas.	Ydem al rescat.	Ganado muerto.
Sonora	„ Seris.			5.				.
Ydem	„ Apaches.	3.	1.	9.	7.			.
Nueva Vizcaya	Apaches	27.		2.	5.	311o.		
Nuevo Mexico	Comanches	1.		86.	34.		5oo.	
Ydem	Apaches	24.		.	.			178o.
Totales		„ 55.	„ 1.	1o2.	46.	311.	5oo.	178o.

Dupp.do}

Arispe 23. de enero de 178o.

De Croix

[7]

N. V.

El dia 13. del corriente se me presentó el Gral
del Piñal Chilitipasé con quatro Capitancillos y sus quadrillas con todo
y familias que son doscientas treinta y seis almas à establecerse
de pie fixo en este lo mismo que los antiguos de paz, los que se
hallan radicados yá en este fabricando sus Xacales para vivir,
y despues de advertido el modo y gobierno con que deben manejarse
arreglado à la instruccion del Sr. Comandante gral. de que quedaron
muy contentos, y al parecer muestran mucha fidelidad, y de que
infiero serán duraderas y estables las pazes que han ofrecid por las
muestras que dán de haber venido con todo y familias, y lo muy
gustosos que están viviendo entre nosotros, à los que estoy racionando
con Reses y la racion acostumbrada de trigo, que el dia que
acavaron de baxar fué el 13, me fué preciso racionarlos à todos
à medio Almud de trigo, para darles el Sábado la que les corresponde
entera; que segun el computo que he hecho para racionar à estos,
y à los antiguos de paz que vienen cada quince dias, se necesita
para los dos meses, mil ciento sesenta fanegas, como lo verá Vm
por diverso oficio. Todo lo que comunico à Vm para su satisfaccion por extraordinario. = Dios que à Vm. m. a. Tucson
Mayo 21. de 1819 = José Romero. = Sr. Comandante de armas
Dn. Antonio Narbona = Es copia Durango 21. de Junio de 1819.
Francisco Velasco = —————————————

Num. 179 = Exmo. Señor = Paso à manos de V. E. original
el adjunto oficio en que el Comandante de la Compañia del Tucson
Teniente Dn. José Romero hace presente haberse establecido de paz
en aquel destino, baxo las condiciones estipuladas, el Indio
Gral del Piñal Chilitipasé con quatro Capitancillos y sus
correspondientes quadrillas, compuestas de doscientas treinta y seis
almas, resultando por conseqüencia en el dia hallarse todas
las Naciones gentiles enemigas, de paz, menos los Yndios
Apaches de la Sierra-blanca, que causan algunas hostilidades
de poca consideracion en el Puesto militar de Bacoachi: lo que
participo à V. E. para su Superior conocimiento. = Dios guarde
à V. E. m. a. Arispe 26. de Mayo de 1819 = Exmo. Señor =
Antonio Narbona = Exc. Señor Comandante gral Dn. Alexo García
Conde. = Es copia. Durango 21. de Junio de 1819 =
Fran.co Velasco = —————————————

Num. 280. = Exmo. Señor = En oficio N. 105. de 10 del pp. Abril
di cuenta à V. E. de los términos en que los Indios gentiles del

[7]

Pinal fronterizos de la Provincia de Sonora se habrian presentado en el Tucsón por medio de su principal caudillo Chilitipagé, y de las prevenciones que hice de como debian ser admitidos. = Por el último correo de linea me há dirigido el Comandante militar de aquella Prov.ᵃ el oficio de que es copia la adjunta, y como de esta y del diverso oficio que cita y tambien acompaño consta que el 13. del pasado Mayo natl Chilitipagé su oferta, presentandose en el expresado Puerto del Tucson con quatro Capitancillos y sus correspondientes quadrillas, compuestas de docientas treinta y séis personas de ambos sexôs: Lo paso todo á manos de V.E. para su inteligencia y satisfaccion; en el concepto de que és la única particularidad que últimamente ha ocurrido en el distrito de las Provincias sujetas á esta Comandancia gral de mi cargo. = Dios gue á V.E. m.ᵃ. Durango 21. de Junio de 1819 = Exc.ᵐᵒ Señor. = Alexo Garcia Conde. = Exmᵐᵒ Sr. Virey Conde del Venadito. = _____

Exc.ᵐᵒ Señor. = Por el oficio de V.E. n.º 280 de 21 de Junio pⁿᵗ y que contesto y copias que lo acompañan, me he enterado de que á consequencia de la paz concedida anteriormente á los Indios del Pinal, se habian estos presentado á vivir con su principal caudillo Chilitipagé en las inmediaciones del Tucson, en número de docienta tres treinta y séis almas. = Dios guarde á V.E. muchos años. México Julio 28. de 1819. = El Conde del Venadito. = _____
Exc.ᵐᵒ Señor Comandante gral de las Provincias internas Ocidentales = _____

Es copia México Julio 31 de 1819

Patricio Humana

Bibliography

ALMADA, FRANCISCO R. *Diccionario de historia, geografía, y biografía sonorenses.* Chihuahua: Ruiz Sandoval, 1952.

Archivo General de Indias. Sevilla, Spain. Copies in the Bancroft Library, Berkeley, California.

Archivo General de la Nacion. Mexico City, Mexico.

BANCROFT, HUBERT HOWE. *History of Arizona and New Mexico.* San Francisco: The History Company, 1889.

_____*History of the North Mexican States and Texas.* 2 vols. San Francisco: The History Company, 1884, 1889.

Béxar Archives. Austin: University of Texas Archives.

BOLTON, HERBERT EUGENE. *Athanase de Méziéres and the Louisiana-Texas Frontier. 1768-1780.* 2 vols. Cleveland: The Arthur H. Clark Company, 1914.

_____*Texas in the Middle Eighteenth Century.* Berkeley: University of California Press, 1915.

CHAPMAN, CHARLES E. *Catalogue of Materials in the Archivo General de Indias For the History of the Pacific Coast and the American Southwest.* Berkeley: University of California Press, 1919.

Civezza Collection. *"Informes de los padres de Sonora, 1772."* Microfilm copy in the University of Arizona Library.

COUES, ELLIOTT T. *The Expeditions of Zebulon M. Pike.* 3 vols. New York: Francis B. Harper, 1895.

DIPESO, CHARLES C. *The Sobaipuri Indians of the Upper San Pedro River Valley, Southeastern Arizona.* Dragoon, Arizona: The Amerind Foundation, Inc., 1953.

FAULK, ODIE B. "A Description of Texas in 1803," *The Southwestern Historical Quarterly,* LXVI (April 1963), 513-515.

_____*The Last Years of Spanish Texas, 1778-1786.* The Hague: Mouton and Company, 1964.

_____"Spanish-Comanche Relations and the Treaty of 1785," *Texana,* II (Spring 1964), 44-53.

GÁLVEZ, BERNARDO DE. *Instructions for Governing the Interior Provinces of New Spain,* 1786 (trans. and ed. by Donald E. Worcester). Berkeley: The Quivíra Society, 1951.

GERALD, REX IRVIN. "A Historic House Excavation Near Janos, Northwest Chihuahua, Mexico" (Unpublished Master's Thesis, University of Pennsylvania, 1957).

KINNAIRD, LAWRENCE. *The Frontiers of New Spain: Nicholas de La Fora's Description, 1766-1768.* Berkeley: The Quivíra Society, 1958.

LUMMIS, CHARLES F. "Some Unpublished History: A New Mexican Episode in 1748," *Land of Sunshine,* VIII (January and February 1898), 74-78, 126-130.

MATTISON, RAY H. "Early Spanish and Mexican Settlements in Arizona," *New Mexico Historical Review,* XXI (October 1946), 273-327.

MINSHEU, IOHN. *A Dictionarie in Spanish and English.* London, 1599.

NEAL, KEITH W. *Spanish Guns and Pistols.* London: G. Bell and Sons, 1955.

PARKE, LT. JOHN G. *Report of Explorations for that Portion of a Railway Route . . . Between . . . the Rio Grande and . . . the Gila,* Vol. VII of *Pacific Railroad Explorations,* Washington, 1853-1856, Sen. Ex. Doc. No. 78, 33rd Congress, 2nd Sess. [Also published as House Ex. Doc.]

PETERSON, HAROLD L. *The Treasury of the Gun.* New York: Golden Press, 1962.

PEDRAZA, GOMEZ. *Decree Establishing and Organizing Presidios for the Defense of the Northern Territories.* Mexico City, 1826 (Copy in the Holliday Collection, Arizona Pioneers' Historical Society, Tucson).

Reglamento para el Ejercito y Maniobras de la Caballeria. Filadelfia, Pennsylvania, 1836 (printed by order of the Government of Mexico; originally published in Spain in 1768. Copy in the possession of Dr. Arthur Woodward, Patagonia, Arizona).

RUSSELL, CARL. *Guns on the Early Frontier.* Berkeley and Los Angeles: University of California Press, 1957.

STEVENS, DON JUAN. *A New Dictionary, Spanish and English, and English and Spanish.* London, 1726.

TAYLOR, VIRGINIA H. *The Letters of Antonio Martínez.* Austin: Texas State Library, 1957.

THOMAS, ALFRED B. *Forgotten Frontiers: A Study of the Spanish Indian Policy of Don Juan Bautista de Anza, Governor of New Mexico, 1777-1787.* Norman: University of Oklahoma Press, 1932.

BIBLIOGRAPHY

_____*The Plains Indians and New Mexico, 1751-1778.* Albuquerque: University of New Mexico Press, 1940.

_____*Teodoro de Croix and the Northern Frontier of New Spain, 1776-1783.* Norman: University of Oklahoma Press, 1941.

WAGNER, HENRY R. *The Spanish Southwest, 1542-1794.* Albuquerque: The Quivíra Society, 1937.

WEBB, WALTER PRESCOTT. *The Great Plains.* Boston: Ginn and Company, 1931.

_____*The Handbook of Texas.* 2 vols. Austin: Texas State Historical Association, 1952.

WOODWARD, ARTHUR. Letters to authors on Spanish uniforms, military equipment, and weapons. January 8, 1964; March 12, 1964. Patagonia, Arizona.

Index

INDEX

This book was manufactured in Arizona. The textual material was set by Linotype in 14-point Old Style Caslon. All typesetting, lithography, and presswork was by the Arizona Messenger Printing Co., Phoenix, with the exception of the title page, set in Codex from Killgore Typesetting Co. The paper is Hamilton's Victorian Text. The binding was by Roswell Bookbinding Co., Phoenix, using Columbia Mills' Riverside Chambray cloth and Oasis morocco.

ARIZONA HISTORICAL FOUNDATION
PHOENIX, ARIZONA